LEARN VISUAL BASIC (VBA)

AND MACROS FOR EXCEL

Author: Josep Ramon Vidal Bosch.

Graphic design: Asnate Cirule

Proofreader: George James Louis Thompson

Book registered in the Territorial Registry of Intellectual Property of Murcia (located at Av. de la Fama, 15, 30006 Murcia (European Union)).

LEARN VISUAL BASIC (VBA)
AND MACROS FOR EXCEL

+ 100 exercises, macros, and games solved to enhance
your programming skills

Josep Ramon Vidal & Bosch

2024

TABLE OF CONTENTS

LIST OF FIGURES

LIST OF TABLES

Prologue

Visual Basic for Applications, also known as VBA, is a programming language used in the Microsoft environment that allows us to create macros and automate repetitive tasks. Using VBA, it is possible to create customized solutions and systematize processes that would otherwise be tedious and error prone.

The aims of this work are three-fold: to understand fundamental concepts of BASIC programming; to design and implement efficient solutions to common problems; and to explore advanced features and techniques to enhance automation capabilities. This book pretends to assist students and professionals in repetitive processes.

The book begins with an overview of computer science and programming, followed by a limited amount of theory. It then provides a significant collection of problems and games to develop skills in VBA applied to Excel.

Throughout, the objective is to guide the reader, step-by-step, from a beginner's level to a position where they can safely and confidently navigate the world of VBA programming for Excel.

Learning VBA is highly recommended for anyone who works with enormous amounts of data and wants to improve efficiency in their workplaces. By using VBA, it is possible to create unique solutions, automate repetitive tasks, and minimize errors, resulting in significant cost and time savings.

Thanks

First, I would like to express my sincere gratitude for the love and patience of my wife, my dear daughter, my parents and I thank God for being able to produce this modest work.

I am also thankful for the knowledge and experience of all the people, colleagues, and friends, who have made it possible for me to learn at the time and for me to be the transmitter of this knowledge today. Their teachings and advice have been fundamental.

Finally, I extend my thanks to the editors and contributors of this book for their tireless efforts in making this project a reality. Their dedication and hard work have made this possible.

To conclude, I regret any disappointment this work may cause and encourage you to contact me (learnVBAforExcel@outlook.com) with any feedback, suggestions, or error corrections.

Thank you for your assistance and support in this endeavor. I trust that this work will be beneficial to you.

1.
COMPUTERS

In modern society, computers are essentials. From our daily routines to the most complex of projects, these electronic devices offer an unprecedented ability to process information and simplify our daily activities. This publication delves into the captivating realm of VBA (*Visual Basic for Applications*) programming, a coding language that empowers users to harness the full potential of MS Excel, one of the paramount office applications in the academic and professional world.

Before delving into the intricacies of VBA, it is important to comprehend the fundamental concepts about computers: their functionality, anatomy, and interaction with them.

Computers are electronic devices capable of receiving, storing, processing, and sending information. They are designed to perform a wide range of tasks, such as word processing, making complex calculations or playing music among many other functions. All of this is possible thanks to its internal workings, designed to process information quickly and efficiently. The wide variety of electronic devices that return outputs to inputs is large, but an electronic device can be considered a computer when it has the following:

- **Hardware** is the physical or visible part of the computer. This expression originates from English language and means "*hard component.*" It contains all the circuitry, including the CPU (*Central Processing Unit*). Hardware would have no utility without input devices (keyboards, mice, sensors, etc.) and output devices (screens, printers, actuators) whereas its others main components consist of an internal memory (RAM and ROM) and an external memory (Hard Disk).

- **Software** is another English term that means *"soft component"* and represents the non-visible part of the computer which comprises all the logic stored in its physical part.

2.
NUMBER SYSTEMS

A number system is a framework of rules adopted to operate with numbers. It is a way to organize and count quantities systematically. Mathematics' groundwork is based on number systems and their usage is applied in a wide range of areas such as computing, physics, engineering, commerce, mathematics, and finance. Several number systems have been employed in various contexts, cultures, and historical moments. Some of them are decimal, binary, octal, hexadecimal, maya or vigesimal system, and others. Of these, we will analyze the decimal and binary systems regarding their significance and relevance to programming.

2.1. Decimal system

The decimal system is a numerical ten-digit system that uses unique symbols to represent numbers. These digits are: 0, 1, 2, 3, 4, 5, 6, 7, 8, and 9.

The decimal system is used worldwide in both everyday life as well as in various domains, such mathematics, finance, science, engineering, and commerce. It is the accepted standard number system for counting, performing calculations, and representing quantities, using the base 10. This is because humans have 10 fingers, establishing it as an instinctive number system. Each time the tenth finger is exceeded, it is said that both hands have been used once. For example, thirteen indicates that both hands and three fingers have been used. Hands would be a primitive type of physical memory.

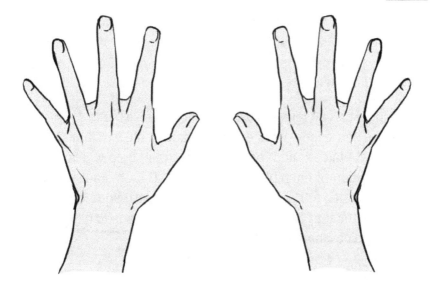

Figure 1. Origins of the decimal system

2.2. Binary system

The binary system is a numerical system that uses only two symbols, known as binary digits, to represent numbers. These digits are 0 and 1. To illustrate, the decimal system is based on multiples of ten, the binary system is based on multiples of two.

The binary system dates back to ancient China and India as early as the third century B.C. However, it was the British mathematician George Boole who, in 1854, provided it as the definitive development with the algebra that we now know as Boolean algebra.

The binary numerical system is essential in electronics and computing since digital devices use electronic circuits that operate using only two states, represented by binary digits 0 and 1. These states were easily recognizable in early computers consisting of several or hundreds of switches and relays, where an open circuit would be read as 0 and a closed circuit as 1.

Currently, a computer memory stores information in binary format consisting of 1s and 0s, commonly referred to as BIT (**Bi**nary Digi**T**).

A BIT is a unit of information that occupies one memory space, represented by either a 1 or a 0. Larger quantities of BITS are named accordingly: for example, a set of 4 BITS is called a "nibble", while 8 BITS are known as an "octet".

A single bit can take two combinations, i.e., a 0 or a 1. The number of values increases with each additional bit, so that 2 bits can produce 4 values and so on. The table below, illustrates the representation of each bit as a letter A, B, C, ..., n. Each letter can be assigned either a 0 or a 1, so they have two unique combinations. This indicates that greater memory capacity leads to higher numbers of possible combinations.

BIT	May take zero	or can take one	Maximum Possibilities
A	0	1	2
B	0	1	2
C	0	1	2
D	0	1	2
E	0	1	2
F	0	1	2
G	0	1	2
H	0	1	2
....	0	1	2
n	0	1	2

Table 1. Explanatory table for 2^n

If each bit in an octet can have two possible combinations, 0 or 1, there will be a total of $2^8 = 256$ combinations when all eight bits are combined. Therefore, the number of combinations needed to remember something is equal to 2^n, where "n" represents the number of bits in our memory equipment.

2.2.1. From decimal to binary

There are several methods for converting a decimal number to binary. To do so, follow these steps:

1. Create a table with three rows and multiple columns. For example, three rows and 7 columns. Large decimal numbers will result in a high number of columns.
2. Then, enter the value 2 in the first row of the table raised to "n" and its decimal equivalent below it. That is, $2^0 = 1$, $2^1 = 2$, $2^2 = 4$, ..., $2^7 = 128$.
3. Then, the number to convert will be broken down into addends that will appear in the table. For example, 14 equals $8 + 4 + 2$. The 24 would be the $8 + 16$.
4. After identifying the sum values, the number one will be placed below and zero will be placed for the unrecognized ones.

2^7	2^6	2^5	2^4	2^3	2^2	2^1	2^0
128	64	32	16	8	4	2	1
0	0	0	0	1	1	1	0

Table 2. Decimal to binary conversion table

So, the 14 in binary would be 1110. The 24th would be 11000.

Try the 106 now. This number is larger than the previous one. So, it can be broken down:

$106 - \mathbf{64} = 42$

$42 - \mathbf{32} = 10$

$10 - \mathbf{8} = 2$

$2 - \mathbf{4} = -2 \rightarrow$ Not acceptable (there are no negatives in the table) so:

$2 - 2 = 0$

2^7	2^6	2^5	2^4	2^3	2^2	2^1	2^0
128	64	32	16	8	4	2	1
0	1	1	0	1	0	1	0

Table 3. Conversion from decimal to binary

So, 106 equals 01101010

2.2.2. Byte

A byte is a measurement unit of information in data storage and processing systems. It is the basic unit of information within computer systems and consists of a fixed number of bits. The number of bits used within a byte has varied throughout history. Early computers utilized bytes which ranged from 6 to 9 bits. However, during the 60s it was determined that 8 bits could handle an adequate amount of information and it became a metric. Since then, within most computers, a byte consists of 8 bits, although certain exceptions exist.

Pre-1998-unit system							
Base	Exponent	Result	Unit	Base	Exponent	Result	
2	0	1,00	B	1024	0	1,00	
2	10	1024,00	KB	1024	1	1024,00	
2	20	1048576,00	MB	1024	2	1048576,00	
2	30	1073741824,00	GB	1024	3	1073741824,00	
2	40	1099511627776,00	TB	1024	4	1099511627776,00	
2	50	1125899906842620,00	PB	1024	5	1125899906842620,00	
2	60	1152921504606850000,00	EB	1024	6	1152921504606850000,00	
2	70	1180591620717410000000,00	ZB	1024	7	1180591620717410000000,00	
2	80	1208925819614630000000000,00	YB	1024	8	1208925819614630000000000,00	

Table 4. Pre-1998-unit system

To understand the above table, consider the first row, where 2 or 1024 is elevated to its exponent, resulting.: $2^0 = 1$, which is equivalent to $1024^0 = 1$. This means that calculations can be made on a base 2, or 1024. Additionally, 1 B (Bytes) = 8 Bits. That is, 1 B = 23 bits (also called an octet, i.e., a byte has eight bits).

The previous methodology changed in 1998 when international system was accepted. Therefore, if a Byte is 8 Bits, a KB is 8000 bits:

$$1 \text{ kB} = 1000 \text{ bytes} = 8000 \text{ bits}$$

Post-1998 numbering system				
kb	1000,00	Bytes	8000,00	Bit
MB	1000000,00	Bytes	8000000,00	Bit
GB	1000000000,00	Bytes	8000000000,00	Bit
TB	1000000000000,00	Bytes	8000000000000,00	Bit
PB	1000000000000000,00	Bytes	8000000000000000,00	Bit
EB	1000000000000000000,00	Bytes	8000000000000000000,00	Bit
ZB	1000000000000000000000,00	Bytes	8000000000000000000000,00	Bit
YB	1000000000000000000000000,00	Bytes	8000000000000000000000000,00	Bit

Table 5. Post-1998 numbering system

2.2.3. Hexadecimal system

The hexadecimal system, introduced by IBM in 1963 is designed to save memory, process information and make programming easier. One advantage of using this system is its ability to represent binary numbers of four digits.

Decimal	0	1	2	3	4	5	6	7	8	9	10	11	12	13	14	15
Hexadecimal	0	1	2	3	4	5	6	7	8	9	A	B	C	D	E	F

Table 6. From decimal to hexadecimal

The hexadecimal system operates on a base-16 alpha-numeric framework. To manually convert a decimal number to a hexadecimal number, divide the decimal number by 16 successively, until the quotient is less than 16. The remainder at each step are replaced by their corresponding hexadecimal digit according to the table above. During calculations skip decimals. When dealing with numbers larger than 9, the hexadecimals digit is represented by letters: A = 10, B = 11, C = 12, D = 13, E = 14, F = 15, etc. For instance, the number 41,716 would correspond to A2F4.

	16	QUOTIENT	REMAINDER	HEX
41.716	16	2.607,25	4	4
2.607,25	16	162,95313	15,~~25~~	F
162,953	16	10,~~18457~~	2,~~953125~~	A2
~~10,1846~~	~~16~~	0,6365356	~~10,18457031~~	-

Table 7. Conversion procedure from decimal to hexadecimal

When the quotient is less than 16 it means that the division process cannot longer continue because the quotient is small enough to be directly converted into hexadecimal digit. At this point, the last quotient obtained and remainder are used.

Finally, all these digits are then arranged in reverse order to obtain the complete hexadecimal representation of the original decimal number.

The inverse procedure involves multiplying each digit by 16x where x is the position of each digit from right to left, beginning with 0. All the resulting values are then summed, resulting in the decimal output.

Example A2F4:

A = 10 → 10 x 163 = 40,960

2 x 162 = 512

F= 15 → 15 x 161 = 240

4 x 160 = 4

Finally: 40,960 + 512 + 240 + 4 = 41,716

The hexadecimal system is employed in various areas of computer science and technology where it is necessary to represent and manipulate binary values in a convenient and compact way. The following section will show some of its applications:

- Programming and development: Facilitating the readability and writing in-memory values, debugging programs, and for memory of addresses.
- Color in graphics and websites: The hexadecimal system is commonly used to represent colors in the field of graphic design and website development. For instance, pure red is represented as #FF0000.
- Cryptography: The hexadecimal system is frequently employed to depict cryptographic keys and data.
- Network addresses: In computer networks, IP addresses are represented using hexadecimal notation
- Editing and viewing binary files: The hexadecimal system is used for executable files, images, and audio.

2.3. Programs & software

A program refers to a collection of organized instructions or code lines designed for accurate and fast computer executions. Software is generally categorized into two broad groups:

- Operating system software which enables computer functionalities.
- Application software that allows the user to carry on with specific tasks such as browsing the Internet, writing documents, or editing images, among many other functions.

The process of creating a program is commonly referred to as programming and entails the use of a **programming language** that consists of a set of instructions. Program development involves the design, coding, testing, debugging, implementation, and its maintenance.

2.3.1. Programming languages

Programming languages enable communication between users or programmers and their computers. Programming languages can be grouped into three main categories:

- *Machine language*: This kind of programming uses a complex binary code which is completely machine dependent. Most programmers find it challenging to program and understand.
- *Low-level language or assembly* language: This language employs mnemonic symbols instead of binary codes. This kind of language must be translated into machine language. Frequently it is used for scheduling critical operating system tasks.
- *High-level language*: It is the closest language to human natural language facilitating comprehension and programming. Notable examples include VISUAL BASIC, Python, JAVA, Kotlin, dart, etc.

To convert high-level or near-human language into machine language, it requires "translators", which can be referred to as interpreters or **compilers.**

Within the high-level language, there are several types of programming languages, each with characteristics and specific uses. However, some of the most used programming languages are object-oriented programming languages:

- **Object-oriented programming languages**: These languages are founded on the concept of object-oriented programming (OOP) where programs are structured as objects that contain data and related functions. Some examples are VBA, Java, C++, Python, Kotlin, Ruby, etc.
- **Scripting languages**: These languages are designed to be small programs or scripts that automate tasks. They are interpreted at runtime.
- **Web programming languages**: These languages are specifically designed for website development, such as HTML, CSS, JavaScript, PHP, others.
- **Mobile App Programming Languages**: These languages are specifically designed for developing apps for mobile devices like smartphones, tablets, smartwatches, and televisions. Examples of such languages are Kotlin, Java, Swift and dart.
- **Visual languages like "Scratch"**: These languages are designed to enhance mental skills for learning programming in a beginner-friendly manner, even without a deep understanding. It utilizes visual elements that operate like a puzzle.

2.3.2. The Algorithm

An algorithm is a procedure that allows the resolution of a computational problem through a set of specific and finite steps.

The origin of the term algorithm could differ depending on the literature consulted. However, several authors agree that the term algorithm originates from the mathematician *Mohamed Ibn Al kow Rizmi*, who wrote, during the period between 800 and 825, his work "*Quitad Al Mugabala*", where he gathered the Hindu system of enumeration and the concept of zero. The text was later translated into Latin as "Algoritmi Dicit" by Fibonacci. According to Royal Spanish Academy of Language, Algorithm would come from the late Latin "algobarismus," which is an abbreviation of the Classical Arabic "hisabu Igubar", signifying calculation with non-Roman numbers. The current numbers (1, 2, 3, 4, 5, 6, 7, 8, 9) were pioneered by the Hindus and further spread by the Arabs.

In any case, algorithms execute repetitive tasks using an ordered and finite sequence of operations, and with a few inputs find the solution of a problem. In general, algorithms have the following characteristics:

- They are precise and accurate.
- They are finite.
- They are repetitive.
- They solve only one problem.
- Its logic can be solved with any programming language.
- They process some entries.

An effective algorithm should have the following characteristics:

- Validity: The code should be error-free.
- Efficiency: The resolution of an algorithm must be fast.
- Optimal: If it is fast and error-free.

The creation of an algorithm consists of several phases:

- Analysis: The problem to be solved is examined, and a solution is proposed.
- Design: The algorithm is developed.
- Test: The outcome is assessed.

Herein lies the difference between artificial or computational intelligence. AI is a tool capable of learning, solving various problems, and using various inputs from its environment. But in this work, at the current level of programming, the inputs are fixed and unique and, the system cannot learn. Consequently, only a single solution can be obtained.

In essence, an algorithm is a sequence of actions or instructions executed in a specific other until the desired solution is achieved. For example, consider the process of picking up a ringing phone: 1. Pick up the phone → 2. Hold the phone to your ear → 3. ask who is calling→ 4. Proceed to have a conversation → 5. When the conversation is finished, end the call by hanging up.

The above steps may seem to a human extremely straightforward and simple and could not deserve any attention. However, scheduling those steps can be arduous work, even days-long work. Therefore, common simple actions such as liking a post on a social network are more complex than they may seem.

2.4. Text and images in the binary system

As mentioned previously, the binary system is an information representation system that uses only two digits, 0 and 1.

These digits are known as bits and are the basic unit of information storage and processing in computers. The combination of bits makes it possible to represent and transmit any type of data, including text and images.

2.4.1. Text

Numbers are easy to convert to the binary, but not text. So, this problem was solved by encoding each character in binary. Each character was a number, and each number was a binary code. The ASCII code can encode up to 127 characters (7 bits):

For example, the capital letter A in ASCII corresponds to the number 65 or 1000001 in binary.

However, a problem arose because this code was sufficient for English language, but insufficient for others. An extension of ASCII was the 32-bit UNICODE code, which made it possible to encode any language in the world.

DEC	OCT	HEX	BIN	Symbol	Description	DEC	OCT	HEX	BIN	Symbol	Description
0	0	0	0	NUL	Null	32	40	20	100000	SP	Space
1	1	1	1	SOH	Start of Heading	33	41	21	100001	!	Exclamation mark
2	2	2	10	STX	Start of Text	34	42	22	100010	"	Double quotes
3	3	3	11	ETX	End of Text	35	43	23	100011	#	Number sign
4	4	4	100	EOT	End of Transmission	36	44	24	100100	$	Dollar
5	5	5	101	ENQ	Enquiry	37	45	25	100101	%	Per cent sign
6	6	6	110	ACK	Acknowledge	38	46	26	100110	&	Ampersand
7	7	7	111	BEL	Bell, Alert	39	47	27	100111	'	Single quote
8	10	8	1000	BS	Backspace	40	50	28	101000	(	Open parenthesis
9	11	9	1001	HT	Horizontal Tab	41	51	29	101001	)	Close parenthesis
10	12	0A	1010	LF	Line Feed	42	52	2A	101010	*	Asterisk
11	13	0B	1011	VT	Vertical Tabulation	43	53	2B	101011	+	Plus
12	14	0C	1100	FF	Form Feed	44	54	2C	101100	,	Comma
13	15	0D	1101	CR	Carriage Return	45	55	2D	101101	-	Hyphen-minus
14	16	0E	1110	SO	Shift Out	46	56	2E	101110	.	Period, dot or full stop
15	17	0F	1111	SI	Shift In	47	57	2F	101111	/	Slash or divide
16	20	10	10000	DLE	Data Link Escape	48	60	30	110000	0	Zero
17	21	11	10001	DC1	Device Control One (XON)	49	61	31	110001	1	One
18	22	12	10010	DC2	Device Control Two	50	62	32	110010	2	Two
19	23	13	10011	DC3	Device Control Three (XOFF)	51	63	33	110011	3	Three
20	24	14	10100	DC4	Device Control Four	52	64	34	110100	4	Four
21	25	15	10101	NAK	Negative Acknowledge	53	65	35	110101	5	Five
22	26	16	10110	SYN	Synchronous Idle	54	66	36	110110	6	Six
23	27	17	10111	ETB	End of Transmission Block	55	67	37	110111	7	Seven
24	30	18	11000	CAN	Cancel	56	70	38	111000	8	Eight
25	31	19	11001	EM	End of medium	57	71	39	111001	9	Nine
26	32	1A	11010	SUB	Substitute	58	72	3A	111010	:	Colon
27	33	1B	11011	ESC	Escape	59	73	3B	111011	;	Semicolon
28	34	1C	11100	FS	File Separator	60	74	3C	111100	<	Less than
29	35	1D	11101	GS	Group Separator	61	75	3D	111101	=	Equals
30	36	1E	11110	RS	Record Separator	62	76	3E	111110	>	Greater than
31	37	1F	11111	US	Unit Separator	63	77	3F	111111	?	Question mark

Table 8. Few examples of ASCII characters

2.4.2. Images

When processing more complex data such as images, video, or audio, encoding becomes much more difficult. There are no international standards for this type of information, as there are for text (ASCII or Unicode). However, there are several ways to encode these file formats. For example, in the case of an image, one way to encode it in binary is to record each of the pixels using three bytes: The first byte stores the red level, the second byte the blue level, and the third byte the green level. This is known as RGB (Red, Green, Blue) encoding. Each component is represented by an 8-bit binary number (also known as a byte), allowing 256 different values to be represented for each component. By combining these three components, an incredible range of colors can be represented in an image.

Another common format for viewing images is BMP (Bitmap), which uses a matrix of bits to represent the pixels in an image. Each bit in the array represents one pixel and can have two values: 0 to represent a black pixel and 1 to represent a white pixel.

Some popular formats for storing, viewing, and transmitting images are JPEG, PNG, GIF, BMP, TIFF, among others. Each format has its own structure and specific rules for storing information such as image size, pixels, color channels, and other associated metadata.

Previous examples are just some cases of how text and images are represented in binary code. The ability to represent information in binary form is fundamental to computer science, allowing a wide range of data to be stored and processed by computers. Today, its study is not finished, and the development of these fields is focused on improvements in visualization, optimization, computational speed, and space reduction in storage devices.

3.
INTRODUCTION TO VISUAL BASIC FOR APPLICATIONS

A computer is a physical device operating through specific input-output mechanisms. The way you interact to this machine vary depending on the machine and its operating system. Computers with Windows operating system provide a language called VBA, implemented in MS Office, to execute commands.

Visual Basic for Applications (VBA) is a secure Microsoft macro programming language[1] which enables the creation of Windows applications. VBA enhance the functionalities of Microsoft Office programs: Outlook, Word, Excel, Access, and PowerPoint.

BASIC stands for *Beginners All-Purposes Symbolic Introduction Code*. The acronym BASIC is derived from its fast-learning curve.

Visual Basic for Applications is a programming language that cannot compile independently from a document, sheet, or database. Additionally, Visual Basic shares similarities with other programming languages such as StarBasic or Open Office.

Keep in mind that Visual Basic is being replaced by the .NET (or C#) programming language, so Microsoft has no plans to make significant improvements to VBA in the future. However, it remains a widely used and supported language within the Microsoft Office system. If you do not have Visual Basic, you can purchase a secure version on the Visual Studio site (.NET compiler).

---

[1] A macro, a term from the Greek and meaning "large". A macro is a set of instructions that allows the automation of repetitive tasks. The macro is stored within the program and can be activated by a key combination, or an icon designated for this purpose. In Windows, VBA is the language to program the macro.

The .NET or C# programming language has similarities to JAVA. Unlike Visual Basic, it enables designing applications for desktop, web, and mobile platforms extending beyond the MS Office environment.

The main advantage of programming in Visual Basic (VBA) is its applicability across a range of scientific, engineering or office discipline in the MS Office environment, facilitating the acceleration of repetitive tasks or data-intensive tasks.

Another benefit of VBA for Excel is its stability. This means that the editor, language, functions and methods do not change massively or recurrently, unlike other languages in which they are deprecated and no longer applicable for the future.

4.
GETTING STARTED IN VBA FOR MS EXCEL

To develop macros and programs in VBA for Excel, one needs to use the VBA editor, which can be found in the 'Developer' menu.

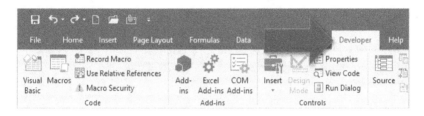

Figure 2. Developer tab location

After, click on the 'Visual Basic' button to open the editor.

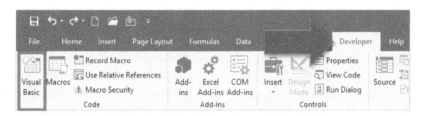

Figure 3. Visual Basic editor for MS Excel

However, the 'Developer' tab may not be visible. If this is the case, you will need to enable it. To do so, navigate to File → Options and then select "*Customize Ribbon*". Then, ensure that the of "*Developer*" box is checked and click "*OK*".

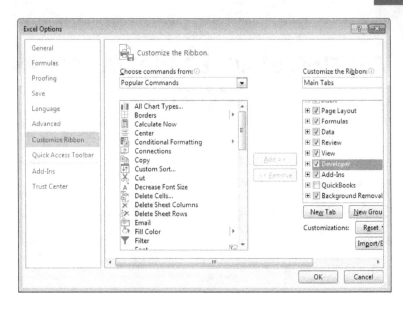

Figure 4. Customizing Excel ribbon

If this option does not appear, navigate to *the "add-ins"* sections in "Excel Options" and enable the "Tools for analysis – VBA" add-in, as shown in the image below.

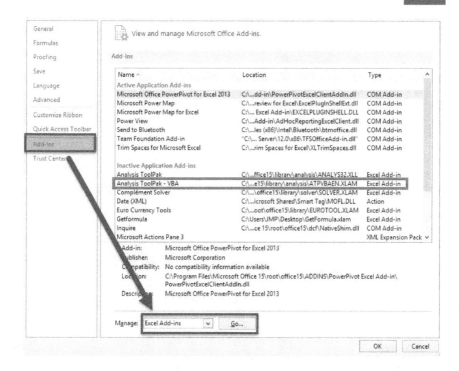

Figure 5. Add MS Excel add-in "tools for analysis"

If everything is right, you can access the VBA editor by clicking on the developer tab. Then, the next tab will be visible.

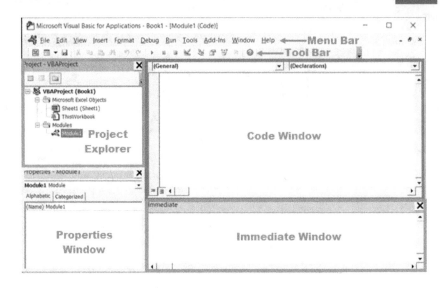

Figure 6. VBA editor for MS Excel

Then, in the editor's "insert" menu, you will find three options: "UserForm", "Module" or "Class Module".

Figure 7. Inserting a new module into the VBA editor

The "UserForm" enables the capability to create dialog boxes for user interactions. Functions and programs can be programmed in the modules, while specific programs for generating custom objects in MS Excel can be created in the class modules.

5.
DECLARING VARIABLES IN VBA FOR MS EXCEL

When beginning to code a program, it is crucial to declare variables. A variable is a memory space reserved by a function or subprocedure for storing data. In general, the way to declare a variable is:

dim *variable_name* as *type*

It is important to specify data type and length. Declaring a variable as an incorrect data type, such as an integer for text, will result in an error in VBA. Additionally, errors can occur if the length or type of data is not properly specified. For instance, if the variable is declared as an integer but the number of bits belongs to a "Long", VBA will throw an error.

Finally, it is recommended to declare all the variables before being used. This way, it will be clear which variables procedure is used and what type of data each one holds. Not declaring variables at the beginning of the procedure have implications: Firstly, VBA assumes these variables as "Variant" types, which can store any value, number, dates, text, etc. but it takes up 20 bytes. Secondly, the readability of procedures is reduced as variables are placed as needed, making it difficult to correct or modify the procedure during execution.

VARIABLES

Type of data	Size	Interval
Byte	1 byte	0 to 255
Boolean	2 bytes	True or False
Integer	2 bytes	-32.768 to 32.767
Long	4 bytes	-2,147,483,648 to 2,147,483,647
Single (Floating Point/Single Precision)	4 bytes	From -3.4028235E38 to -1.401298E-45 for negative values; 1.401298E-45 to 3.4028235E38 for positive values.
Double	8 bytes	From -1.79769313486232E308 to -4.94065645841247E-324 for negative values; 4.94065645841247E-324 to 1.79769313486232E308 for positive values.
Currency (integer to scale)	8 bytes	-922.337.203.685.477.5808 to 922.337.203.685.477.5807
Decimal	14 bytes	+/-79,228,162,514,264,337,593,543,950,335 without decimal point; +/-7,9228162514264337593543950335 with 28 positions to the right of the decimal mark; The smallest non-zero number is +/-0.0000000000000000000000000001
Date	8 bytes	January 1, 100-31, 9999
Object	4 bytes	Any reference to type Object
String (variable length)	10 bytes + string length	From 0 to 2,000 million
String(fixed length)	Chain Length	From 1 to approximately 65,400
Variant(with numbers)	16 bytes	Any numeric value up to the range of a type of Double
Variant(with characters)	22 bytes + string length	The same interval as for a variable-length String type
User-Defined (Type)	Number required by the elements	The range for each item is the same as the range for its data type.

Table 9. Summary of data types

5.1. Option explicit

Option Explicit is a VBA checker that returns an error if some variables are not declared. It forces the variables to be declared and prevents potential compilation errors. *"Option explicit"* must be specified prior to any other line of code. When "Option *Explicit On"* or *"Option explicit"* statement is used in a code, it is mandatory to explicitly declare all variables using the "Dim" or *"ReDim"* statements. If a variable is undeclared, and attempts are made to use it, then it will fail at compile time. The *"Option explicit Off"* statement allows inference of variables, meaning that the VBA infers the type of each variable.

To enable the *explicit option* in the VBA, go to Tools → *Options* and there, under *"Require Variable Declaration"*.

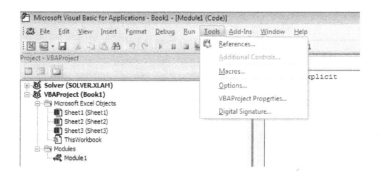

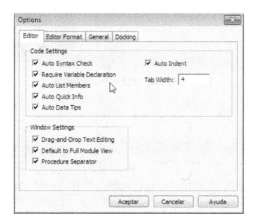

Figure 8. Activation of the "option explicit"

6.
HIERARCHY IN VBA PROGRAMMING

VBA for MS Excel is an object-oriented language that has its own syntax with a mandatory hierarchy that must be understood. This hierarchy goes from highest to lowest. This is particularly important when working with different sheets in Excel. The programming hierarchy in VBA generally follows the following structure:

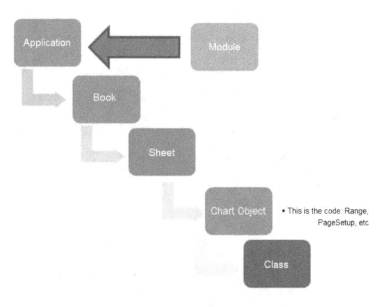

Figure 9. Hierarchy in scheduling

The top-level object is the "Application" and represents the Excel sheet. In most cases, it is not necessary to explicitly reference the Application object, because all objects depend on it. However, if macros or code are used across multiple workbooks or files, it may be necessary to reference the Workbooks object.

7.
MACROS IN MS EXCEL

An Excel macro is a tool that enables recording and playback of a sequence of commands or instructions in Microsoft Excel. Macros automate repetitive or complex tasks, making it easier to process large amounts of data or perform specific actions more efficiently.

Excel records all actions performed within the spreadsheet in a Macro, including cell formatting, formulas or functions used, copy, and paste operations, and more. The macro can be run to automatically perform all these actions, instead of having to manually repeat them. Excel macros are useful in a variety of situations, including:

- Task automation: Performing repetitive tasks, such as formatting a table, creating reports, generating charts, or updating data.
- Data processing: Macros can also help with large volumes of information by automating data cleaning, filtering, sorting, or analysis.
- Customization of functions: Customized functions can be generated to extend the functionalities of Excel and adapt it to specific needs.
- Interaction with other applications: Macros enable interaction with other Microsoft Office applications, such as Word, PowerPoint, or Access, to exchange information or perform combined actions.

7.1. Record a macro

The most straightforward method of creating a macro in Excel is by using the macro recorder. This tool enables you to record the desired actions and translates them into VBA instructions, which can be modified later (modify macros).

The macro recorder saves all the actions you performed manually on the worksheet or worksheets. After pressing the save macros button, Excel starts recording the code of all the actions you perform, such as selecting, transposing, and changing the font.

Figure 10. Recording macro icon

To record a macro, navigate to the "*View*" tab and display the "*Macros*" submenu. From there, select the "*Record Macro*" option. The '*View Macros*' option can also be found in this menu, which will allow you to access a list of all macros created in your document.

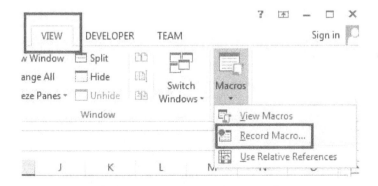

Figure 11. Accessing to Excel's VBA "record macro" button

The third option, known "relative references," enables macros to record actions relative to the selected starting cell.

Macros can also be saved from the "Developer" tab. If this tab is not available, follow the steps outlined in the chapter 'Getting Started in VBA for MS Excel'. To summarize, click on the Microsoft Office (or File) button and then select Excel options.

Figure 12. Excel options icon

Then navigate to "Excel options" and select the "show programmer tab" option in the "ribbon". Finally, click "OK":

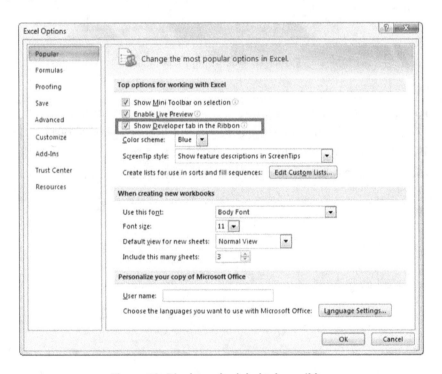

Figure 13. Display scheduled tab on ribbon

Depending on the Office version, navigate to Excel Options, select "Customize Ribbon", and click on the "Check Box" of Developer. Then press OK.

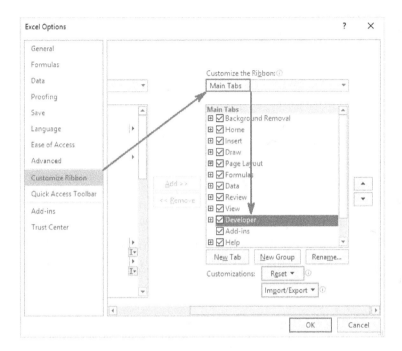

Figure 14. Excel options

After completing this task, the Excel interface will be updated in the following manner:

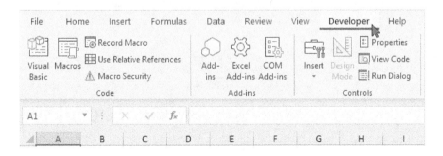

Figure 15. Developer menu

Then you can be ready to record macros:

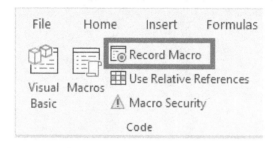

Figure 16. Icon "Record Macro"

7.2. Macro name

When naming a macro, be aware that no special characters, reserved words, or spaces are allowed. In this case, you can use an underscore ("_") as a word separator, or you can use a notation such as camelCase.

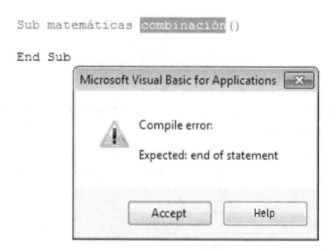

Figure 17. Common mistakes

In the example above, an error appears when attempting to name a macro as *"matemáticas combinación"* or *"matemáticas_combinación"*.

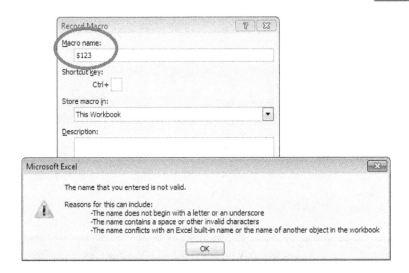

Figure 18. Common mistakes when naming a macro

In the previous case, it is observed that a macro cannot be named as "$123", and advise that:

- The name does not begin with a letter or an underscore.
- The name contains a space or other invalid characters.
- The name conflicts with an Excel built-in name or the name of another object in the workbook.

7.3. Security in macros

To adjust the security level, follow these steps; First, navigate to the "Developer tab" and locate the "Code group". Then, click on "Macro Security" and follow the instructions provided:

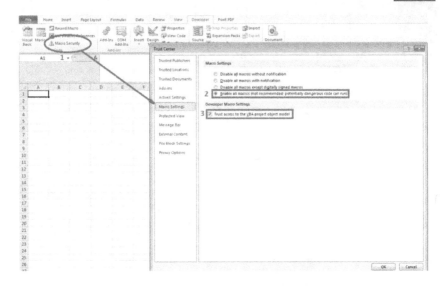

Figure 19. Macro's security options

Under "Macro Settings", click "Enable all macros" ("not recommended; potentially dangerous code can be executed") and then click OK. Please be aware that a macro with malicious intent has the ability to completely wipe and damage your computer.

It is important to note that leaving these options activated can leave your computer vulnerable to malicious macros. When downloading Excel sheets from the internet, be cautious as they may contain harmful code that can damage your computer.

To prevent potentially dangerous code from running, it is advisable to undo the changes in the settings and disable all macros once you have finished working with them.

8.
THE FIRST PROGRAM: "HELLO WORLD"

The "Hello World" program is the most basic program that can be created, and its unique purpose is to print the text: "Hello World" on the screen through an alert window or in a cell.

It is often used as an introductory program to familiarize users with programming of one specific language.

The most probably origin of this program is in the book *"Programming with the C Language,"* from 1978 which was based on an internal Bell Labs document from 1974 written by Professors *Brian Kernighan* and *Martin Richards*.

There are several ways to create the 'hello world' program. However, the two simplest methods are: displaying an alert message (pop-up window) or showing the text 'hello world' in a cell.

8.1. Displaying 'Hello world' in a pop-up window.

The following is a basic program that displays a 'hello world' message in a pop-up window or alert. Copy the following code into a module and run the program:

Figure 20. The "Hello World" program in a pop-up window

8.2. Displaying 'Hello world' in a cell

Like the previous program, this program also displays the text "hello word". However, it is done in a cell instead of pop-up window. To run the program, enter the following text into a module:

Figure 21. The "Hello World" program in a cell

Also, it is possible to write the "Hello world" in a specific active cell, using the code bellow. The text is enclosed in quotation marks ("") to indicate that it is a string.

```
Sub hello_world()
        Range("A2").Select
        ActiveCell = "Hello_World"
End Sub
```

9.
PARAMETERS AND ARGUMENTS

When working with functions, procedures, and subprocedures in Excel VBA, it is crucial to distinguish between parameters and arguments. Although both concepts are similar, they have subtle differences.

- Parameter: A parameter is a value that a function or subroutine (Function or Sub) expects to **receive** parameters are also used as placeholders for values that are sent as arguments. Parameters are defined in the header of the function or subroutine and can have a name, an associated data type, a pass-through mechanism (ByRef or ByVal), or if it is an optional parameter (the call is not required to send you a value).
- Argument: An argument is the value or data that is **passed** to a function or subroutine. This is the value assigned to the corresponding parameter in the call to the function or subroutine. Arguments can be variables, constants, or expressions that have the type of data expected by the parameter. Arguments lack names and can contain zero, literal, constant, or variable.

The parameter can be thought of as a mailbox and the argument as a letter. The letter represents the argument, and the mailbox represents the parameter. Each time a letter is sent, it will arrive in the designated mailbox.

10.

THE AUTOINCREMENTALS

Auto-incrementals allow the automatic generation of sequential values without user intervention. Autoincremental programming is a highly useful instruction. The expression of autoincremental is:

$$c = c + 1$$

In other programming languages, the above statement can be simplified by c++, but it is not possible to do so with VBA, using ++ operator is not available in this language.

The above autoincremental does the following:

One assumes nullity, i.e., 0.

- $c = 0 + 1 = \rightarrow 1$. Save 1 and enter it on the next line.
- $c = 1 + 1 = \rightarrow 2$. Save 2 and enter it on the next line.
- $c = 2 + 1 = \rightarrow 3$. Save 3 and enter it on the next line.
- $c = 3 + 1 = \rightarrow 4$. Save 4 and enter it on the next line.
- ....And thus, up to the desired upper limit.

Note that, the first "c" in the first iteration is assigned to 0 because nothing existed before. Additionally, you can assign 'c' to any other value, which is one of the advantages of programming and Excel. A typical Excel sheet without macros is static. This means that when working on a "normal" sheet you can only repeat the calculations once unless you update the values, with Ctrl + Alt + F5. However, with VBA, you can iterate as much as you need.

11.
RECOMMENDED NOTATION TYPE IN VBA FOR MS EXCEL

In programming language, notation style refers to the set of rules and conventions used to name variables, functions, constants, and other elements in code. These conventions define how names should be written and structured to ensure readability and comprehension for both developers and readers.

Notation styles may include capitalization, spacing, underscores, or other characters to separate words, and the use of descriptive and meaningful names. There are various types of notations commonly used in programming, including camelCase, pascalCase, snake_case, and kebab-case.

In VBA programming language for MS Excel, it is recommended to use the *camelCase notation*. This notation style involves starting each word with a capital letter, except for the first word, which begins with a lowercase letter.

This notation style enhances code readability and comprehension by clearly separating words and capitalizing each word except the first one.

Although camelCase is the recommended style, some developers may prefer other styles, such as using underscores to separate words (e.g., animal_name) or alternative notation styles.

Regardless of the coding style used, it is crucial to maintain consistency throughout the code to ensure readability and ease of understanding for the programmer, collaborators, and future self.

12.

VBA PROCEDURES AND SUB-PROCEDURES FOR MS EXCEL

A module's code is organized into procedures and sub-procedures. Sub-procedures, such as 'Sub workOffice()', teach the application how to perform specific tasks. Procedures and sub-procedures are used to break down complex code into more manageable parts.

The difference between procedures and sub-procedures lies in whether the code returns a value or not.

12.1. Characteristics of a Subprocedure in Excel VBA

A subprocedure is a set of instructions that performs a specific task but does not return any value. Subprocedures are primarily used to execute actions and perform tasks without the need for a specific outcome.

- The program subprocedure begins with the Sub statement and ends with the End Sub statement.
- Any text preceded by an apostrophe (') is considered a comment and will not be executed by the compiler. Comments are displayed in green.
- Subprocedures are designed to perform specific tasks without returning any results, although output or reference parameters can be implemented.

12.2. Characteristics of a Procedure in Excel VBA

Procedures and functions are a set of instructions that perform a specific task, but unlike subprocedures, they return a value. Functions are used when a return value is required elsewhere in the code.

- Procedures or functions are preceded by the reserved keyword "function".
- If an explicit return value is not specified for a function, it returns the default value for the declared data type. For example, a function declared as Integer without an explicit return value will return the default value of 0.

12.3. Public Procedure

In VBA, a public procedure is a procedure that is accessible by all procedures in all modules of a project.

```
Public Sub procedure_name(optional: argument1, argument2, etc....)

          < Instructions >
End Sub
```

Note: By default, VBA defines a procedure as public. This means that if you do not write "*Public*" and only "Sub", VBA will interpret it as a public procedure.

12.4. Private Procedure

A private procedure is a procedure that can only be accessible by other procedures within the same module. Its syntax is as follows:

```
Private Sub procedure_name (optional: argument1, argument2, etc....)

        < Instructions >
End Sub
```

Note: Private procedures are used on forms and certain functions.

12.5. Static Procedure

It is a type of procedure that enables variables to be retained even after their execution is complete.

```
Static Sub procedure_name(optional: argument1, argument2, etc....)
        < Instructions >
End Sub
```

13.
VBA CLASSES IN MS EXCEL

Classes are the set of instructions that are written within "class modules", allowing VBA to generate objects. Objects are created from classes and have methods and properties.

In modern languages such as C#, Kotlin, Java, etc., classes are used to create objects. However, VBA class modules have limited inheritance compared to classes in other languages. In VBA, inheritance works similarly to interfaces in C# or Java.

VBA has pre-existing objects such as a collection, workbook, and spreadsheet. The purpose of VBA "*Class Modules*" is to enable the construction of custom objects.

- Inheritance uses an existing class to create a new class.
- Interfaces are a type of inheritance that forces a class to implement specific procedures or properties.

13.1. Objects and Properties of a Class

By default, VBA includes a wide range of predefined objects such as spreadsheets, charts, cells, forms, and reports. They are predefined objects. However, by using classes, it is possible to create custom objects. Objects can be compared to tangible, physical entities. Imagine that a person is an Excel object. The properties of the subject would include the color of their eyes, the color of their hair, and their height.

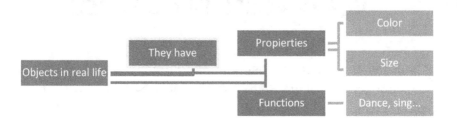

Figure 22. Objects, properties and functions in real life

In non-virtual contexts, an object refers to a tangible entity that can take various forms, such as a car, pencil, chair, balcony, or house, etc. The **house class,** for instance, represents all houses worldwide by defining their common features, such as walls, windows, roof, and base. Any physical structure with walls, a roof, and windows can be classified as a house. Some Excel-specific objects:

- WorkSheet.
- Range (Object, cell, or range of cells).
- A graph.
- Comments in a cell.
- A pivot table.

It is common that the property of one object can be another object. For instance, in the example of a car, the engine is one of its many properties. The engine has properties such as power, number of cylinders or valves, etc. In object-oriented programming, classes use functions, referred to as methods. The methods of the car class would include increase_rpm, refill_fuel, move_pistons, etc. In MS Excel, the Worksheets("Sheet1") object has the Range property, which is also an object. The Range object, in turn, has a Font property (another object) and a Bold one.

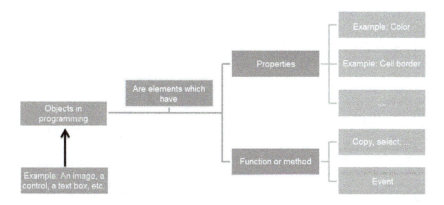

Figure 23. Object types in VBA

In object-oriented programming, objects can have properties, which can also be objects themselves, forming a hierarchy.

In VBA, by clicking on the object browser in the toolbar: you will notice that at the bottom there is a window divided into two parts. The left side displays the class, which groups the members (on the right), including objects, properties, functions, and others.

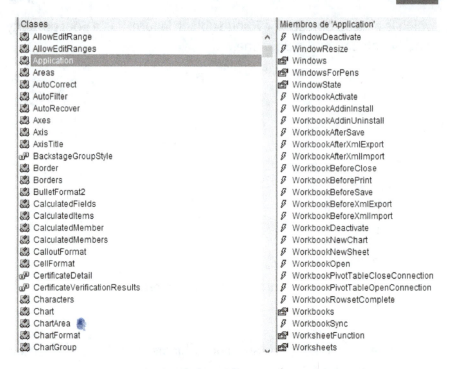

Figure 24. Examples of classes and members

In summary, the use of objects enables the creation of applications using building blocks.

Each object's code is autonomous and independent of any other code in the application, similar to building with LEGO or TENTE bricks.

These toys have a wide variety of components. For example, a block, a steering wheel, and a window are different elements. The components operate independently of each other. For example, the wheel rotates and the window allows light to pass through. However, when combined, they can form structures such as buildings, vehicles or rockets.

13.2. Advantages of Using Objects

Treating parts of the code as blocks offers significant advantages.

- It is much easier to evaluate individual parts of an application.
- Updating the code will not cause problems in other parts of the app.
- Additionally, it is easy to add objects between apps.

13.3. Disadvantages of Using Objects

Like many things in life, there are both advantages and disadvantages to using VBA class modules to create objects. The following are the disadvantages:

- The time required to generate an application is greater.
- Defining an object is not always a straightforward task.
- Novice programmers may struggle to understand the concept of a class.
- Creating an application using objects requires a greater initial investment of time and planning for design. However, in the long run, it can save time and money due to easier code management, updates, and reuse.

13.4. Properties

An object has various characteristics or properties such as color, shape, weight, dimensions, etc. These properties are defined within a class and then instantiated on each object. For instance, in the car class, properties such as color, width, and height can be defined. Subsequently, when defining an object as a car, these properties would be specified as: Color = green, width = 5.5 meters and length = 8.5 meters. Some of the most frequently occurring properties are:

- Value
- Cell Name
- Valid address of an active cell
- Number of sheets in the workbook

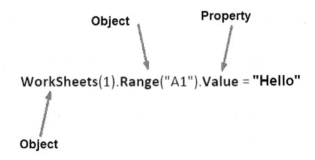

Figure 25. Objects and properties

The full stop "." is used to separate the object from the property, just as it is used to separate an object from a method. For example, in the following case you have the object "WorkSheets("sheet1") with the property "Name".

Worksheets("sheet1").name = "Hello!"

13.5. Creating a Class Module

When generating a new standard class in VBA for MS Excel, there is the option to implement properties using the Let and Get procedures or using public variables instead.

To create a class module, right-click on the Project window, and select Insert and Class Module.

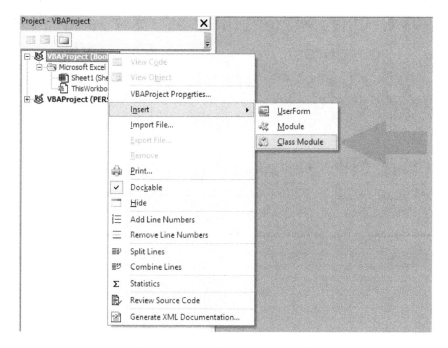

Figure 26. Inserting a class module

The newly created class has been named Class1. The name can be modified in the Properties window as shown in the following screenshot:

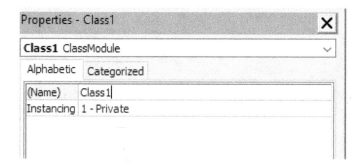

Figure 27. Editing the class name

The desired name is then assigned, for instance, 'NewClass'.

13.6. Class without the "Let", "Set", and "Get" Procedures

In this simple method, the instance sends the arguments to a sub-type class module.

13.6.1. Code to be inserted in the standard module

In this way of generating a new class, use a public variable, instead of the Let, Set, and Get properties.

```
Sub test()
        Dim hello As New newClass
        hello.sayHello("Hello!")
End sub
```

13.6.2. Code to be inserted in the class module

```
' This is a new class named "newClass"
Public name As String

Sub sayHello (user As String)
        name = user
        MsgBox ("¡Hello " & name)
End Sub
```

To instantiate a class, use the following instruction in the standard module:

```
Dim hello As  New NewClase
```

NewClass is the name of the class, set in the module's properties. If you look at it, "hello" behaves like a variable. Also, notice that in front of the new variable is the reserved keyword *"Dim"*. That is, "hello" is a variable of type NewClass.

13.7. Creating a Class with the "Let" and "Get" Properties

Unfortunately, the simplest approach mentioned above is not always the most advisable. As a rule, public variables within a standard class should be avoided, and instead, the keyword 'private' should be used. Additionally, it is preferable to use the methods, *"Let"*, *"Set"* and *"Get"*. This is because these properties provide benefits such as encapsulation, internal state maintenance, interoperability, and event support. All of these features contribute to more robust, modular, and easy-to-maintain code:

13.7.1. In the module

```
Sub test()
        Dim hello As New newClass

        hello.sayHello = "Hello World!"
        msgBox (hello.sayHello)
End sub
```

13.7.2. In the Class Module

```
Private name As String
```

```
Public Property Let sayHello (nm As String)
        name = nm
End Property
```

```
Public Property Get sayHello() As String
        sayHello = name
```

End Property

One of the advantages of a class is that you can use it as many times as you need:

```
Sub test()
        Dim hello As New newClass
        Dim hello2 As New newClass
        Dim hello3 As New newClass

        hello.sayHello = "Hello World"
        hello2.sayHello = "Hello World 2"
        hello3.sayHello = "Hello World 3"
        msgBox (hello3.sayHello)
End Sub
```

13.8. Parts of a Class Module

The examples above provide a generic analysis of the concept and components of a class.

1. **Class Statement:** Every class must have a name.
2. **Attributes or instance variables:** After declaring the class, the attributes are defined using variables. These attributes are specific to each class and are referred to as "instance variables." For example: Private myVariable as Integer.
3. **Methods**: Methods are functions within classes. They define the behavior of the class and can access and manipulate, the class attributes while performing operations.
4. **Properties**: These functions behave as variables. They include the Let, Set, and Get functions.
   a. Get = returns or extracts the value of the object.
   b. Let = inserts the value inside the object.
   c. Set = if applicable, configures the object. Creates the value of a property that references an object.

5. **Events**: These are Subs that are automatically executed when an event occurs, they consist of two parts: Class_Initialize() and Class_Terminate().

There are three fundamental aspects that distinguish a standard module from the class module.

1. In a standard module, the data is shared by all parts of the program that use it. This means that if a variable is declared in a standard module, its value will be the same in all instances that access it. In contrast, in a class module, a separate copy of the data is created for each instance of the class. Each instance of the class has its own set of individual class variables to the object, which means that each instance can have different values for those variables.
2. In a standard module, the data exists for the duration of the VBA. However, in a class module, data only exists for the lifetime of the class object. When the class object is destroyed (for example, by setting the object to Nothing), the data associated with that instance of the class is also deleted. Each instance of the class can have its own dataset that is independent of other instances.
3. Public variables declared in a standard module are visible and accessible from anywhere in the VBA project. They can be used and modified by any module, form, or object on the project. However, public variables in a class module are only accessible if you have an object variable that contains a reference to a particular instance of that class. This means that public variables in a class module can only be accessed through a specific instance of the class. Public variables in a class module cannot be accessed directly without a reference to an object in that class.

To work properly with a class module, it is important that each class has its own module, which should be renamed to reflect the object's customization.

13.9. Rectangle exercise

Calculate the area of a rectangle with dimensions 3 x 4 units

This exercise is interesting because it enables the user to send the length of each side as arguments and returns the area of the figure.

13.9.1. Main standard module

```
Sub test()
        Dim calculation As New newClass
        calculation.calculate 3, 4
End Sub
```

13.9.2. Class Module

```
'This is a new class named "newClass"
Public x As Double
Public y As Double
Public area As double
_____

Sub calculate(x As Double, y As Double)
        area = x * y
        msgBox (area)
End Sub
```

13.10. Smartphone Example

The following example define the features of a smartphone like brand, model, and memory capacity. The Let and Get properties will be used to create this example.

13.10.1. In the Class Module

```vba
Private myBrand As String
Private myModel As String
Private myMemory As Double


'Property brand
Public Property Let brand(Value As String)
   myBrand = Value
End Property


Public Property Get brand() As String
   brand = myBrand
End Property


'Property model
Public Property Let model(Value As String)
   myModel = Value
End Property


Public Property Get model() As String
   model = myModel
End Property


'Property Memory
Public Property Let Memory(Value As Double)

   ' Check if number has been inserted
   If IsNumeric(Value) Then
     ' With ABS (Absolut), the number is always positive.
      myMemory = Abs(Value)
      Else
        ' If the input is not a number, the value is set to null.
        myMemory = 0
```

```
    End If
End Property
```

```
Public Property Get Memory() As Double
    Memory = myMemory
End Property

Public Sub calling()
    ' Our code
    MsgBox " I have used the model to make a call " & model
End Sub
Public Sub SMS()
' Our code
MsgBox " I have sent an SMS message from this phone " & Memory & "GB"
End Sub
```

```
Sub Data()
' Our code
MsgBox "Data is consumed using the brand's phone " & brand
End Sub
```

13.10.2. In the standard module

```
Sub testingTelephone ()
Dim telephone As New newModuleClass
            telephone.brand = "Nokia"
            telephone.memory = 20
            telephone.model = "S9"
            telephone.calling
            telephone.data
            telephone.SMS
            Set telephone = Nothing
End Sub
```

There are three interesting features in this program: sending a value to the class, calling a method of the class, and destroying an object. To dissociate a real object from an object variable, the reserved keyword 'Nothing' is used.

13.11. Methods

Methods typically perform operations on objects. In general, objects exhibit behaviors or carry out actions. For instance, the primary action of the car object is to move from one point to another. In VBA for Excel, you can either use default methods or create your own.

- Activate
- Clear
- Copy
- Select
- ClearContents

To avoid errors, it is recommended to refrain from mixing methods and properties. For instance, attempting to activate a cell and assign a value simultaneously will result in failure.

```
Sub hello()

        Range("A1").Activate.Value = 10

End Sub
```

To prevent VBA from highlighting errors in yellow, it is necessary to separate methods and properties as indicated above:

```
Sub hello()

        Range("A1").Activate
        Range("A1").Value = 10

End Sub
```

13.11.1. Accessing objects, methods, and properties

An object's properties and methods are accessed through point notation (.). For instance, to access the 'Value' property of a cell, type 'Range("A1").Value'.

VBA provides an autocomplete and contextual help while writing code, making it easy to explore and select appropriate methods and properties.

14.
USERFORMS

A UserForm is a custom window or dialog box created using controls that respond to specific actions. To add a UserForm, follow these steps:

1. Press Alt + F11 to access the Visual Basic editor or go to the VBA editor and right-click on the project explorer area and add a UseForm. If the project explorer is not visible, proceed to the next step.

2. Enable the following options:

- From the View Menu, select the "Project Explorer" option
- In the View Menu, select the "Properties Window" option

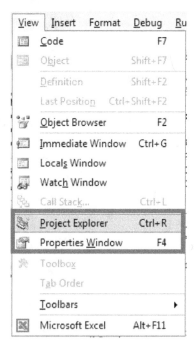

Figure 28. Project explorer and property window

3. To insert the form to be programmed using controls, select the UserForm option from the Insert menu. The Project Explorer will then show the insertion of the UserForm.

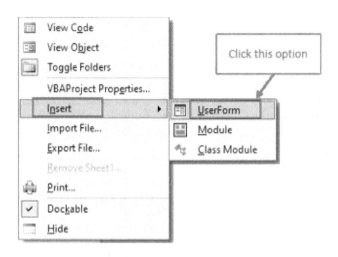

Figure 29. VBA UserForm

When clicking on Form USERFORM1 the Toolbox should be activated. If not activated, click on the View Menu and select the Toolbox option.

4. After determining the desired interface and its necessary actions, select one of these available options:

- Label
- Text box
- Combo Frame
- List Box
- Checkbox
- Radio Button
- Toggle button
- Frame
- Command button
- Tab bar
- Multi-Page
- Scroll bar
- Number button
- Image
- RefEdit

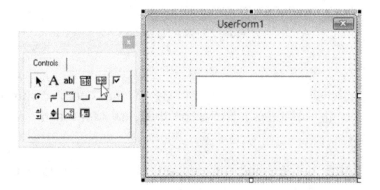

Figure 30. Creating a UserForm

The sizes and positions of the different options can be adjusted, and their names can be modified to facilitate identification during coding.

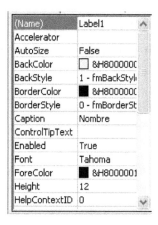

Figure 31. Modifying a label in VBA

To modify options in the Properties Window, it is necessary to have knowledge of the controls' properties and avoid altering any unknown properties. For instance, a potential UseForm could be:

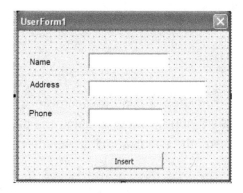

Figure 32. Result of a UserForm

To begin programming after creating the UserForm, double-click on the desired control (e.g., button, checkbox, textBox, etc.) within the form. This action will open the code editor with the header and the end of the code. Once the UserForm is coded, activate it by clicking on the 'Run UserForm' button in the toolbar or by pressing the F5 key to run the code.

14.1. Closing an UserForm with a button

To close a UserForm window using a 'Cancel' button, use the following code:

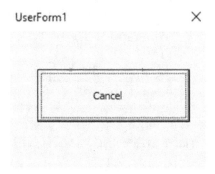

Figure 33. Example of a simple UserForm

```
Private Sub CommandButton1_Click()
 End
End Sub
```

This exercise provides a simple example of a UserForm. Its purpose is to close a pop-up window using the cancel button. Upon running the program, the window will close when the cancel button is pressed.

14.2. Example of a drop-down list using a "combobox"

To create a drop-down menu with a list of items, select the following code:

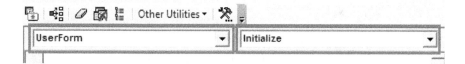

Figure 34. VBA ComboBox

To add the desired elements, select 'UserForm' and 'Initialize' from the drop-down menu at the top. Follow these steps:

```
Private Sub UserForm_ Initialize ()
          With GARANTIA
                    .AddItem "YES"
                    .AddItem "NO"
          End With
End Sub
```

This feature enables additional actions to be performed on the selected item. When an item is chosen from the list, a new drop-down menu will appear.

```
Private Sub drop_ Change ()
ga = Me.drop.ListIndex

          If ga = 0 Then
          myItems.myList.Visible = True
          End If

          If ga = 1 Then
          myItems.myList.Visible = False
          End If

End Sub
```

14.3. Refedit

REFEDIT control is a tool available in the toolbox form, commonly used to insert data ranges for tables and formulas. To use the Refedit control, navigate to the VBA editor and right-click in the Project Explorer area, and add a UserForm. Once the UserForm is added, you can find the RefEdit control in the toolbox and place it on the UserForm for further use.

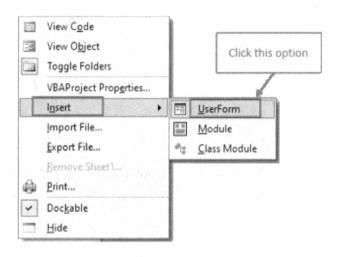

Figure 35. Embedding a UseForm in VBA

To access the Refedit, right-click on the 'Toolbox' and select 'additional controls'.

Figure 36. Inserting additional controls

Then the following window will appear. Select "Refedit":

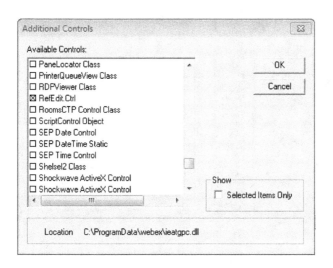

Figure 37. Additional controls of type RefEditCtrl

You will then notice the following icon in the toolbox:

Figure 38. RefEdit icon

Providing an example, we will analyze how interesting the RefEdit is. So, look at this example about how to sum up a set of cells, just by selecting them.

To do so, create a UserForm with a Refedit and an "OK" button. Then, double-click on the OK button (1).

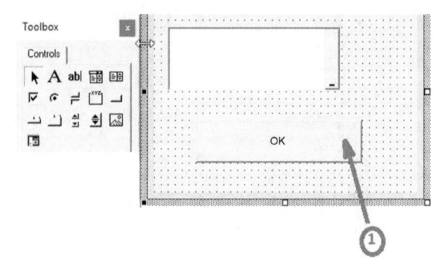

Figure 39. Creating a UserForms

Then, the editor will open with the following instructions:

```
Option Explicit
```

```
Private Sub accept_click()
End Sub
```

Between Private Sub and End Sub, add the following code:

```
Private Sub accept_click()
        Dim a As String
        Range("A1").Clear
        A = RefEdit1.Value
        Range("A1").FormulaLocal = "=sum(" & a & ")"
End Sub
```

Then, press run ▶. A pop-up window will appear. The Refedit will be filled with the selected cells before press the "OK" button, and the sum will be made.

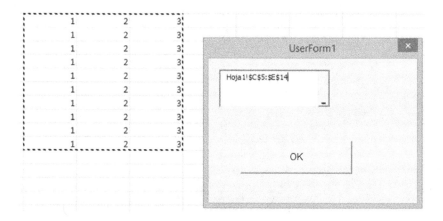

Figure 40. Sum of selected cells

15.
TIME MEASUREMENT IN VBA FOR MS EXCEL

In VBA for MS Excel, time is primarily managed using the "*Date*" objects and their associated functions and properties. The 'Now' property is commonly employed to retrieve the current date and time, whereas the 'Time' function displays the present time without including the date."

1. To get the current date and time

```
Sub myTime()

  MsgBox Now

End Sub
```

2. Get the Current Time

```
Sub myTime()

  MsgBox Time

End Sub
```

3. Format dates and times

```
Sub myTime()

  MsgBox Format(Now, "dd/mm/yyyy hh:mm:ss")

End Sub
```

4. Convert a string to a "Date" object:

```
Sub myTime()

  Dim myHour As Date
  myHour = TimeValue("10:30:05")

End Sub
```

15.1. VBA chronometer for Excel

As for the chronometer, VBA does not provide a specific function to create a real-time timer. Nevertheless, you can employ the previous mentioned functions to measure the time for specific tasks or operations.

If you wish for a chronometer in a particular cell (e.g., in the worksheet1), you can use the following code. This code serves as a timer, updating every second.

```
Option Explicit
_____

Sub auto_open()
          myTime
End Sub
_____

Sub myTime()
          Worksheets("sheet1").Range("A1").Formula = Now()
          Application.OnTime Now + TimeValue("00:00:01"), "myTime"
End Sub
```

If the time is not displayed correctly, select the cell, and go Home → Time → Number format. This will allow you to see the seconds ticking by.

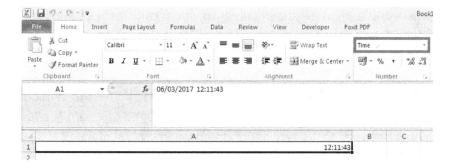

Figure 41. Stopwatch with VBA

15.2. Moving an active cell every second

Another interesting exercise is to go down one row every second. The problem is similar to the previous one and can be solved using the following code.

```
Option Explicit

Sub auto_open()
        myTime
End Sub


Sub myTime()
Dim t, a As Integer
  t = Second(Now())
  Range("A1").Value = t
  Application.OnTime Now + TimeValue("00:00:01"), "myTime"

  If t >= 0 Then
    a = 1
  End If

ActiveCell.Offset(a, 0).Select

End Sub
```

The application begins at sub auto_open() and invokes sub time(). In "time", two variables are declared to store the values. The time unit used is seconds.

First, the value of 't' is displayed in cell A1. If "t >= 0" (which is always true), the value a = 1 goes down. Since the program is a loop, "a" will be equal to 1 every second and will move by one cell.

16.
THE WITH

The "With" statement is a tool that executes a package of instructions without having to refer to the same object, avoiding repeating code, increasing its clarity, and increasing the speed of routine executions. Its syntax is as follows:

```
With Object
            ... Instructions (...)
End With
```

An interesting and explanatory example of the "With" concept:

```
With ActiveSheet
            . Range("A1"). Value = Product
            . Range("A2"). Value = Price
            . Range("A3"). Value = Quantity
            . Range("A4"). Value = Total
End With
```

In the example provided, the 'ActiveSheet' object was only mentioned once instead of four times. Another instance of its use is demonstrated below:

```
Set MyCell = WorkSheets(1). Range("B5")
            With MyCell
                        . MyCell.Value = 12
                        . Font.Bold = True
                        . Font.Italic= True
End With
```

17.
CALL A PROCEDURE

VBA for MS Excel's typically uses a concept called 'calls' to organize, sort, and reuse code by using smaller, more specific procedures and sub-procedures. This concept improves readability, maintainability, and the ability to work in larger teams. Some of the advantages are:

- Modularity: Breaking down code into smaller procedures and sub-procedures enables addressing and focusing on specific problems individually.
- Code reuse: The use of calls enables the writing of a code block and using it in multiple sections of the program, preventing redundancies and enhancing the performance and consistency of development.
- Readability: By breaking down the code into smaller, more specific procedures and sub-procedures, it becomes more readable and understandable. This also enables other programmers to quickly comprehend the code without having to study the entire program.
- Maintainability: When making code changes or corrections, it is easier to do so by using small, individual procedures rather than searching for and modifying scattered code throughout the program.
- Facilitate teamwork: When working in teams of developers, breaking down code into procedures and sub-procedures can facilitate collaboration. This allows each developer to focus on their respective procedures before integrating them into the main program.

Therefore, procedure calls aid in improving the organization, readability, maintenance, and reusability of the code, enhancing its efficiency and quality. The simplified diagram below illustrates that when a procedure calls another, the former yields its execution to the second to returning after and to finish its own execution.

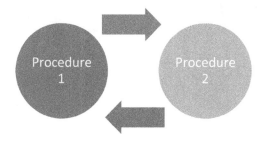

Figure 42. Procedural calls

To invoke a procedure from another procedure, the reserved word "*Call*" can be used optionally. In the given example, a subroutine named "first" is defined which displays two messages: "*This is the first*" and the second: "*This is the second.*" The first procedure calls the second, executes it, returns to the first, and issues the last message. The following two examples perform the same function, one without and the other with the reserved keyword "Call":

Sub myExample()
  First
MsgBox "This is the second"
End Sub
	Sub myExample()
	  Call First
	MsgBox "This is the second"
	End Sub

Sub first()
  MsgBox "This is the first"
End sub
	Sub first()
	  MsgBox "This is the first"
	End sub

For instance, consider the multiplication of two numbers, 'a' and 'b', using a function.

```
Option Explicit
```

```
Sub myCode()
        MsgBox multiplication(2.4, 7.3)
End Sub
```

```
Function multiplication(a, b)
        multiplication = a * b
End Function
```

The structure is as follows:

```
Sub procedure_name()
        < Instructions >
    Call function_name/subprocedure (argument 1, argument 2, argument 3,
etc.)
        < Instructions >
End sub
```

```
Sub Procedure (Parameter1 as Type, Parameter2 As Type, ..., Parameter3 As
Type, etc.)
        < Instructions >
End sub
```

It is important to ensure type matching in the parameters. This means that if the first parameter is a variable of type Integer, the first value passed to the procedure when it is called must also be an Integer type.

18.
MOST COMMON INSTRUCTIONS

Here are the most common instructions to be used in Excel VBA.

18.1. Select a Cell

```
Range("A1"). Select
```

18.2. Writing in an active cell

```
Activecell.Value ="Agata"
```

18.3. Bold letter in selected cell

```
Selection.Font.Bold = True
```

18.4. Italics in the selected cell

```
Selection.Font.Italic = True
```

18.5. Underlined letter in the selected cell

```
Selection.Font.Underline = xlUnderlineStyleSingle
```

18.6. Centre Text in the selected Cell

```
Selection.HorizontalAlignment = xlCenter
```

18.7. Align Left in selected Cell

```
Selection.HorizontalAlignment = xlLeft
```

18.8. Align right on selected cell

```
Selection.HorizontalAlignment = xlRight
```

18.9. Font in the selected cell

```
Selection.Font.Name = "Agata"
```

18.10. Font size

```
Selection.Font.Size = 15
```

18.11. Copy method

```
Selection.Copy
```

18.12. Paste method

```
ActiveSheet.Paste
```

18.13. Cutting method

```
Selection.Cut
```

18.14. Sort ascending

The following code sorts column A in ascending order, once selected, with a header in A1.

```
Selection.Sort Key1:=Range("A1"), Order1:=xlAscending, Header:=xlGuess, _
OrderCustom:=1, MatchCase:=False, Orientation:=xlTopToBottom
```

18.15. Descending order

The following code sorts column A in descending order once selected, with a header in A1.

```
Selection.Sort Key1:=Range("A1"), Order1:=xlDescending, Header:=xlGuess, _
OrderCustom:=1, MatchCase:=False, Orientation:=xlTopToBottom
```

18.16. Find

The following code searches for the word hello throughout the spreadsheet and hovers over it.

```
Cells.Find(What:="hello", After:=ActiveCell, LookIn:=xlFormulas,
LookAt:=xlPart, SearchOrder:=xlByRows, SearchDirection:=xlNext,
MatchCase:= False). Activate
```

18.17. Insert/Add row

```
Selection.EntireRow.Insert
```

18.18. Delete row

```
Selection.EntireRow.Delete
```

18.19. Insert column

```
Selection.EntireColumn.Insert
```

18.20. Delete column

```
Selection.EntireColumn.Delete
```

18.21. Open a book

Workbooks.Open Filename:="C:\My documents\my.xlsFile"

18.22. Record a book

ActiveWorkbook.SaveAs filename:="C:\My documents\mio.xls", FileFormat:=xlNormal, password:="", WriteResPassword:="", ReadOnlyRecommended:= false, CreateBackup:=False

18.23. Calculating the integer from a division

Use the back slash: WorkSheets("sheet1"). Range("A1"). Value = 10 \ 7

18.24. Calculate the remainder from a division

Use the "mod" to find the residue: Worksheets("sheet1"). Range("A2"). Value = 10 Mod 3

18.25. Length of a cell

If you want to know the number of digits in a certain cell or value, you can use the "Len" method.

- **Value:** Worksheets("sheet1"). Range("A2"). Value = LEN("1000")
- **Cell:** If you want to know the length of a piece of data inserted into a certain cell:

```
Option Explicit


Sub myLength()
        Dim e As String
        e = Range("A1").Value
        Worksheets("sheet1").Range("A2").value = Len(e)
End Sub
```

18.26. Lookup

In Excel VBA, the "Vlookup" method is used to find a specific value in a range of cells and returns the location of the first occurrence of that value:

```
Option Explicit

Sub mySearch()
        Dim myData As Integer
        myData = Application.VLookup("Searched_Value";
Range("$A1$1:$B$10"), 2, False)
        MsgBox myDate
End Sub
```

18.27. Create Excel sheet with VBA

```
Worksheets.add.name = "Agata"
```

18.28. Delete a sheet in Excel

For example, if you want to remove "sheet2" from the workbook, then:

```
Sub delete_sheet2()
    On error Resume Next
    Sheets("sheet2").delete
End sub
```

The use of *'On error resume next'* prevents compilation errors in case 'sheet2' does not exist. Later, we will analyze the complexity of error handling. In this other example, the code checks if "sheet 1" exists, and if so, delete it:

```
If Worksheets(1).Name = "sheet1" Then
   Sheets("sheet1").Delete
End If
```

18.29. Delete all cells on an entire sheet

To erase the entire contents of a sheet, the following code can be used.

```
Sub delete_information()
      Worksheets(1).Cell.Clear
End Sub
```

18.30. Hide/Show spreadsheets

18.30.1. To hide:

In VBA for MS Excel, cells can be hidden by using the 'Hidden' property for a given object, such as rows or columns. For instance:

```
Sub Hide()
     Range("1:1").EntireRow.Hidden = True
     Range("A:A").EntireColumn.Hidden = True
End Sub
```

18.30.2. To display:

On the other hand, if you wish to display the previously hidden rows and columns, change from "true" to "false":

```
Sub show()
     Range("1:1").EntireRow.Hidden = False
     Range("A:A").EntireColumn.Hidden = False
End Sub
```

Then, to display a previously hidden sheet:

```
Sub show_sheet()
    Worksheets(1).Visible = True
End Sub
```

18.31. Select a range into a loop

Sometimes, it may be necessary to select rows or columns within a 'for' loop. This can be achieved by:

```
Worksheets("sheet1").range(cells(2,b), cells(1345, b)). Select
```

18.32. Count range on non-empty cells

```
Application.WorksheetFunction.CountA("G:G")
```

18.33. Copy a cell from "A1" to "B1" in the same Excel sheet

Copy cell A1 of "sheet 2" to cell B1 of "sheet 2".

```
Option Explicit

Sub copyPaste()
   Worksheets("sheet2").Range("A1").copy
   Worksheets("sheet2").Range("B1").PasteSpecial xlPasteAll
   Application.CutCopyMode = false
End Sub
```

18.34. Copy rows & columns from one to another sheet

```
Sub copy()
Range("A1:D10000"). Copy → Copies the range of cells from A to D. That is,
                            the upper vertex A1 to the lower right
                            vertex D10000.
Worksheets("sheet2"). Range("A1:D10000"). PasteSpecial xlPasteAll PasteAll Paste → the
                            range of cells from A to D. That is, from
                            the upper vertex A1 to the lower right
                            vertex D10000.
Application.CutCopyMode = False
End Sub
```

18.35. Copy column from A to column B

```
Range("A:A"). Copy destination:=range("B:B")
```

18.36. Copy row from row 1 to row 2

```
Range("1:1"). Copy destination:=Range("2:2")
```

18.37. Copy from cell A1 to cell B1 on sheet3

```
WorkSheets("sheet3"). Range("A1"). Copy
destination:=WorkSheets("sheet3"). Range("B1")
```

18.38. Copy from cell A1 on sheet2 to cell B1 on sheet3

```
Worksheets("sheet2"). Range("A1"). Copy
destination:=WorkSheets("sheet3"). Range("B1")
```

18.39. Locate the position of the active cell

The position of the active cell can be determined using the following function:

- ActiveCell.Row
- ActiveCell.Column

In this example, cells A1 and A2 will display the position of the active cell every time the program runs.

```
Option Explicit


Sub positionCell()

   Range("A1").Value = ActiveCell.Row
   Range("A1").Value = ActiveCell.colum

End Sub
```

18.40. Jump from one cell to another cell

The offset function enables scrolling through a spreadsheet, similar to using the arrow keys on a keyboard.

- ActiveCell.Offset(0,0). Select: Don't move. Remains in the same active cell.
- ActiveCell.Offset(1,0). Select: Move down one row.
- ActiveCell.Offset(-1,0). Select: Move up a row. Do not switch columns.

- ActiveCell.Offset (2,-1). Select: Move down two rows and see a column to the left.
- ActiveCell.Offset(-3,4). Select: Move up three rows and see four columns to the right.
- ActiveCell.Offset(-1,1). Select: Move up a row, and you see a column to the right.
- ActiveCell.Offset(1,-1). Select: Move down a row, and you see a column to the left.
- ActiveCell.Offset(-1,-1). Select: Move up a row, then move a column to the left.
- ActiveCell.Offset(1,1). Select: Move down a row and turn a column to the right

18.41. Last number of a column

To determine the final value of a data list, use the following code, being interesting with the "for" loop:

```
Range("A1").value = Range("B" & Rows.Count). End(xlUp). Row
```

18.42. Create a filter with VBA

To implement the filter with VBA, first select the worksheet:

```
Sheets("sheet1"). Select
```

Then select the filter row:

```
Rows ("2:2"). Select
```

To filter the data, select the criteria you want to filter. For instance, you can filter column 20 based on the whitespace criterion and values within the range of B2 to U8000.

```
ActiveSheet.Range("$B$2:$U$8000"). Autofilter Field:=20, Criteria1:="="
```

Note 1: Filter out worthless or blank cells: "="
Note 2: Filter out cells that contain values (not blank cells): "<>"
Note 2: Contains a certain value. For example, if you want the unit value: "1"

18.43. Coloring cells with VBA

There are various methods to change the color of cells in Excel. One of these methods is to use the "ColourIndex" method, which allows you to choose from one of Excel's 56 present colors. To change the color of an active cell, you can use the following code:

```
ActiveCell.Interior.ColourIndex = 36
```

To change the color of a range of cells, you could use this instruction:

```
Range("A1:A6"). Interior.Colour = RGB(200, 160, 27)
```

The difference between the ColourIndex and RGB properties lies in the act that the former has 56 predetermined colors. RGB, on the other hand, enables choice of infinite variations in the spectrum of red, green, and blue colors to achieve a specific shade.

Observe with this simple code, the 56 colors mentioned above that Excel is capable of "painting" with its default colors:

Option Explicit

```vb
Sub colorIndex()
    Dim i As Integer
    Cells(1, 1).Value = "index"
    Cells(1, 2).Value = "color"

    For i = 1 To 56
        Cells(i + 1, 1).Value = i
        Cells(i + 2, 2).Interior.colorIndex = i
    Next i

End Sub
```

Index	color	Index	color	Index	color	Index	color
0	Neutral	14		28		42	
1		15		29		43	
2	White	16		30		44	
3		17		31		45	
4		18		32		46	
5		19		33		47	
6		20		34		48	
7		21		35		49	
8		22		36		50	
9		23		37		51	
10		24		38		52	
11		25		39		53	
12		26		40		54	
13		27		41		55	

Table 10. Color palette using the "ColourIndex"

In the previous color palette, the "0" represents the absence of color, i.e., the default white of the cells. The "2" represents the white color itself and both can appear identical in one cell.

18.44. Highlight the active cell

To change the active cell to a specific color, insert this code into ThisWorkbook:

```
Option Explicit


'Code inside of "ThisWorkbook"
Public lastCell As Range
Public lastColor As Long

Private Sub workbook_open()
    lastColor = ActiveCe11.Interior.Color
    Set lastCell = ActiveCe11
End Sub


Private Sub workbook_sheetSelectionChange(ByVal sh As Object, ByVal target
As Range)
On Error Resume Next

    lastCell.Interior.Color = lastColor
    lastColor = ActiveCell.Interior.Color
    ActiveCell.Interior.Color = RGB(153, 204, 0)
    Set lastCell = ActiveCe11
End Sub


Private Sub workbook_beforeSafe(ByVal saveAsUI As Boolean, cancel As
Boolean)
    lastCell.Interior.Color = lastColor
End Sub
```

18.45. Number of cells in a range

To count the number of cells in a column list, use the following code:

```
a = Worksheets("sheet1"). Range("A" & Rows.Count). End(xlUp). Row
```

It can be especially helpful when, for example, there is a 'For' available and a list range from j = 2 until the end.

18.46. Minimum and maximum of a range

To calculate the minimum and maximum range of any column, use the following functions:

```
Minimum = Application.WorksheetFunction.Min(Worksheets("Sheet1").
Range("F:F"))
Maximum = Application.WorksheetFunction.Max(Worksheets("Sheet1").
Range("F:F"))
```

18.47. Number of days between two dates

To calculate the number of days between a start date and an end date, use the following function:

```
days = Application.WorksheetFunction.Days(EndDate, StartDate)
```

18.48. Number of repeated cells in a range

Use the following instruction to count the number of repeated cells in column B, excluding the header. A "for" loop is required:

```
Option Explicit

Sub countIf()

    Dim i, finalRow As Integer
    finalRow = Worksheets("Sheet1").Range("B:B").End(xlUp)

    For i = 2 To finalRow
        Cells(i, 1).Value =
Application.countIf(Worksheets("Sheet1").Range("B:B"), Cells(i, 2))
    Next i
```

```
End Sub
```

19.
API PROGRAMMING

This type of programming is used when it is necessary to use external applications that cannot be directly integrated with EXCEL. An API, which stands for Application Programming Interface, is used to run and close external applications from Excel.

For example, if you want to display the current temperature of a particular city in an Excel cell, you can use an API to obtain the information, which is not available by default in MS Excel. For instance, an external company's API like OpenWeatherMap can be used. To use it, a free key must first be obtained from the OpenWeatherMap website (https://openweathermap.org → "Sign up" → Register → Generate API keys"). After obtaining the key, go to the code editor (accessible directly with Alt + F11) and select the Tools → menu → select the references and find the box for "*Microsoft WinHTTP Services*". Then, select References and find the box for "*Microsoft WinHTTP Services*".

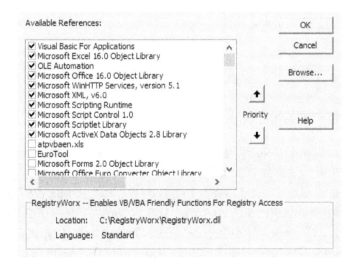

Figure 43. Required references for using APIs in VBA for Excel

Some of the above references may be useful when working with JSON, which is a common format for APIs. Please insert the following code into the editor:

```
Option Explicit

Sub getClimaData()

  Dim apiKey As String
  apiKey = "7XXXXXXXXXXXXXXXXXXXXXXXXid"

  Dim city As String
  city = "La Pobla de Segur"

  Dim url As String
  url = "https://api.openweathermap.org.data/2.5/weather?q=" & city &
"appid = " & apiKey

  Dim http As Object
  Set http = CreateObject("MSXML2.XMLHTTP")
  http.Open "GET", url, False
  http.send

  Dim answer As String
  answer = http.ResponseText
  Range("A1").Value = answer

End Sub
```

Getting the following information in cell A1:

{"coord":{"lon":0.9667,"lat":42.25},"weather":[{"id":800,"main":"Clear", "description":"clearsky","icon":"01n"}],"base":"stations","main":{"temp":2 81.97,"feels_like":280.66,"temp_min":281.97,"temp_max":281.97,"pres sure":1020,"humidity":50},"visibility":10000,"wind":{"speed":2.38,"deg":2 1,"gust":2.24},"clouds":{"all":2},"dt":1680474131,"sys":{"type":2,"id":2004 983,"country":"ES","sunrise":1680500153,"sunset":1680546169},"timez one":7200,"id":3113298,"name":"la Pobla de Segur","cod":200}

The temperature is "temp: 281.97" and is referenced in degrees Kelvin. To convert it to °C, subtract 273.15. That is, 280.6°K − 273.15 = 7.45 °C This is expected as it is a high-altitude location in the middle of the Pyrenees during autumn. In addition, a function can be created to extract and display the relevant data in the desired location in a spreadsheet.

This is a simple example of how to use an API in VBA for Excel. APIs are commonly used for automating tasks and retrieving information from external sources.

For instance, when sharing your GPS location with a friend through certain commercial applications, you are actually calling an API from Google Maps or another commercial platform. In simple terms, an API enables two applications to communicate and share information in a concrete manner.

APIs have many advantages. When, for example, a courier company adds a geolocation service, it typically uses an API rather than creating its own. This ensures a higher quality service as the API is provided by a company dedicated to this task.

In the following example, a random qualifier about cats is retrieves from an external website to MS Excel, without the need for API key. To do this, enter the following code:

```
Option Explicit
```

```
Sub getCatFact()
Dim xhr As New MSXML2.XMLHTTP60
Dim url As String
Dim answer As String
Dim done As String
Dim start As Long
Dim finish As Long

    url = "https://cat-fact.herokuapp.com/facts/random"
    xhr.Open "GET", url, False
    xhr.Send
```

```
answer = xhr.ResponseText
start = InStr(answer, "text"":""") + 7
finish = InStr(start, answer, """", vbBinaryCompare)
fact = Mid(answer, start, finish - start)
Range("A1").Value = done

End Sub
```

When working with APIs, it is crucial to prioritize security measures to safeguard sensitive data and prevent unauthorized access. This includes protecting API keys from exposure, implementing secure authentication methods such as OAuth, and validating user input to prevent injection attacks. Additionally, regularly updating and patching APIs to address vulnerabilities is essential for maintaining a secure environment. By adhering to best practices in API security, organizations can minimize the risk of data breaches and ensure the integrity of their systems.

20.
EVENTS IN EXCEL VBA

Events in VBA are procedures that are executed because of a user action or program code, such as pressing a key or opening a workbook. Excel VBA events allow you to control and respond to different actions that occur within a spreadsheet or in the Excel environment in general.

1. Events in the spreadsheet: Events in the spreadsheet are triggered when specific actions occur within the sheet, such as changing the value of a cell or when saving an Excel workbook.
2. Workbook events: These events pertain to the Excel workbook. They are triggered when a specific worksheet is opened or closed, or when other actions are performed within the workbook.
3. Application events: These events are related to the Excel environment. They are triggered when Excel is opened or closed, when an action is performed on the toolbar, or when an option is changed in the settings.

To enhance comprehension of this tool, consider the following example where a message will appear in a pop-up window upon opening a spreadsheet.

To ensure the message appears upon opening the workbook, the event must be applied to the entire workbook. Therefore, the event will be written in the 'ThisWorkbook' section.

Figure 44. ThisWorkbook in the project tree

A drop-down list will then appear and select Workbook:

Figure 45. Workbook selection

Then, to the right, a second drop-down menu will appear, allowing you to select your desired option.

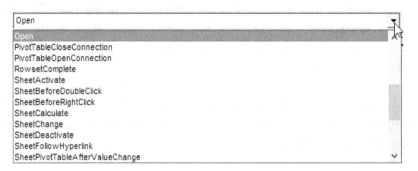

Figure 46. "open" the list of properties and methods

Then select 'Open'. This will enable an action to be performed upon opening the workbook. When the event is selected, the following lines will be automatically typed: *Private Sub workbook_Open()* .... End Sub. Between these lines, write the desired instructions. In this case, a message.

```
Private Sub workbook_Open()

        MsgBox "Hello World"

End Sub
```

Finally, save the code and workbook, close the spreadsheet, and then reopen it. The box below should appear:

Figure 47. Pop-up with a "Hello World"

20.1. OnKey Method: Application.OnKey(key, procedure)

The "OnKey" method is part of the Excel object library and executes a specific procedure on an active sheet, when a particular key or key combinations are pressed, i.e., it captures keyboard events. The basic syntax is:

Application.OnKey(key, Procedure)

Name	Required/Optional	Type of data	Description
Key	obligatory	String	A String indicating the key to be pressed.
Procedure	Optional	Variant	A String indicating the name of the procedure to be executed. If the procedure is "", then nothing happens when the key in question is pressed.

Table 11. OnKey Method. Key and procedure

The key can be activated by a combination of ALT, CTRL, SHIFT, or directly through the desired key.

It should be noted that when using the "OnKey" method, you should ensure that you have any key association disabled at the end of the code or when you do not need to capture keyboard events. This is especially important if you are sharing the file with other users or if you want to maintain the behavior of the Excel keys.

20.2. Example of OnKey

Type the number 1 in "A1" by pressing the "s" key

If you run the following code and press the letter "s", you will be able to see how the number 1 is written in the "A1" cell.

```
Sub assign()
        Application.OnKey "s", "write1"
End Sub

_____

Sub write1()
        Worksheets("sheet1").Range("A1").Value = 1
End Sub
```

21.
THE LOOPS

Loops are a control structure that enables a block of code to be repeated a specific number of times. This tool is particularly useful when you want to execute a series of instructions iteratively until a certain condition is met. There are several types of loops:

- For type loops
- C loops

21.1. "For" – "Next"

The For-Next loop is a commonly used and useful loop in VBA. It enables the repetition of a set of instructions for a specific number of times, with control over the start, end, and step of each iteration.

```
For initialization To limit variable
            Instructions
Next
```

For instance, increment from 1 to 1000 one at a time by adding the successor to the previous number. Unless otherwise specified, the initial value is i = 0.

```
For i = 1 To 1000

        i = i + 1
Next
```

This is equal to:

- 1 = 0 + 1
- 2 = 1 + 1
- 3 = 2 + 1
- 4 = 3 + 1

etc.

Examine another use case for the 'for-next' loop by performing an exercise that concatenates the cells of columns A and B into column D.

```
For i = 1 to 100
        Range("D" & i). Value = Range("A" & i). Value & Range("B" & i).
Value
Next
```

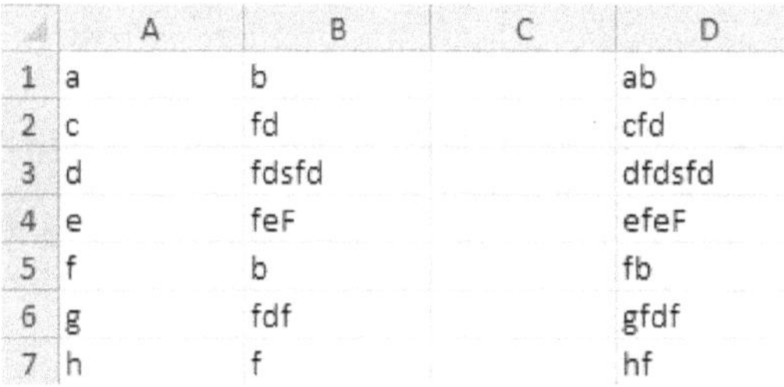

	A	B	C	D
1	a	b		ab
2	c	fd		cfd
3	d	fdsfd		dfdsfd
4	e	feF		efeF
5	f	b		fb
6	g	fdf		gfdf
7	h	f		hf

Figure 48. Example of cell concatenation

21.2. The "For - Each" Instruction

The term 'For-Each' refers to performing an action on each item in a collection or array. This allows for the manipulation of a set of objects of the same type, such as cells, sheets, books, files, and graphical objects. The For Each [XXXX] in [YYYY] statement can be used to repeat a set of instructions for each item in the collection or array.

- [XXXX] → **Group element:** This is required and refers to each of the objects to be worked with. (MyCell)
- [YYYY] → **Group:** This is the name of the group set. (the selection)

The Exit For statement is optional. It is often used in expressions such as 'If... then' to allow for exiting the loop.

The example below demonstrates how to color multiple cells within a specific range, using a maximum of 56 colors.

```
Sub paint()

   For Each cell In Range("A1:A56")
     a = a + 1
     cell.Interior.ColorIndex = a
   Next

End Sub
```

This example enables the user to change the name of each sheet to a new name specified in cell A1.

```
Option Explicit

Sub sheetName()

   For Each mySheet In ThisWorkbook.Worksheets
     mySheet.Name = mySheet.Range("A1").Value
   Next

End Sub
```

This example illustrates how to calculate the sum of cells in an integer selection.

```
Option Explicit
_____

Sub example()

   For Each myCell In Selection
     Sum = Sum + cell.Value
     ActiveSheet.Range("E1").Value = Sum
   Next

End Sub
```

21.3. The "Do" loops

"Do" loops are a type of repetitive structure that enable the execution and iteration of a set of instructions until a specific condition is met. In the field of programming, these fundamental structures are commonly referred to as loops, iterations, or other similar terms.

Repetitive structures often use counters or self-increments, accumulators, loop outputs, and jumps. Here are some examples:

- Counter or autoincrement: c = c + 1, c = c − 1. In other languages it is c++ or c--.
- Accumulator: c = c + x, j = j − i.
- Exit the loop: *"Exit Do"* or *"Exit For"*.
- Continue to the start of the Do While loop and For: "Continue".

Do loops can be classified into four main types:

a) DO WHILE − LOOP: If the initial condition is met, the loop will repeat. The instructions are executed first, and then the condition is evaluated. If the condition is false, the loop will terminate.
b) DO - LOOP WHILE: If a condition is met, the calculations are repeated from the beginning. The loop is executed at least once.

c) DO - LOOP UNTIL: The loop is executed at least once and repeats the calculations from the beginning until a condition is met.

d) DO UNTIL - LOOP: This construct is like a 'Do While' loop, but it continues to repeat until a specific condition is satisfied.

The distinction between them lies in the location of the loop's start and end points. In (a), nothing happens until the condition is met, which is located at the beginning. In (b), the condition is located at the end, and the loop runs at least once if the condition is met. In (c), the loop is executed only once before exiting.

21.4. "Do While - Loop" instruction

Repetitive procedures that use the "for-loop" are appropriate when the number of times a process must be repeated is known in advance. For example, when counting ten values, going through fifty cells or thirty rows, etc. However, there are situations when the exact number of times a process should be repeated is unknown. For instance, if you need to iterate through a set of rows where the number of values is unknown (i.e., the number of complete rows is uncertain), such as ten, twenty, none, etc., the "for-loop" may not be the best option. Instead, it is recommended to use the "Do While" statement... Loop in one of its forms. The repetition of the instruction block is dependent on one or more conditions controlling this type of repetitive structure.

```
Do While
        <instruction1>
        <instruction2>
        <...>
        <Instruction N>
Loop
```

To comprehend these concepts, you can execute the following simple problem in the VBA editor. An iteration will run only if a specific condition is met.

```
Sub exampleDoLoopWhile()

  Dim myCounter As Integer
  myCounter = 1

  Do While myCounter <= 5
    MsgBox myCounter
    myCounter = myCounter + 1
  Loop

End Sub
```

In the example provided, a counter is used to keep track of the number of iterations. At the end of each iteration, the initial condition is evaluated. The C loop will continue to run as long as the initial condition remains true.

21.5. Do-Loop While Instruction

The repetitive structure operates similarly to the previous one, with the exception that the condition is evaluated at the end. As a result, the instructions in the loop body will be executed at least once. The following example illustrates this concept:

```
Sub exampleDoLoopWhile()

  Dim myCounter As Integer
  myCounter = 1

  Do
    MsgBox myCounter
    myCounter = myCounter + 1
  Loop Until myCounter <= 5

End Sub
```

21.6. Instruction Do... Loop Until (until the condition is fulfilled)

The "Do... Loop Until" is a repetitive structure that evaluates the condition at the end. It is important to note that the loop repeats until the condition is met, not while it is met.

The above example would be modified as follows:

```
Sub exampleDoLoopWhile()

    Dim myCounter As Integer
    myCounter = 1

    Do
       MsgBox myCounter
       myCounter = myCounter + 1
    Loop Until myCounter > 5

End Sub
```

As is clear, this example is like the previous one, although with some subtle differences.

- Do-Loop While: Execute the instructions if the condition is less than to 5.
- Do-Loop Until: The instructions will stop executing when the condition is greater than 5.

21.7. Do Until – Loop Instruction

This type of "Do-loop" will continue running until the condition is true. Once the condition is met, the loop will exit and proceed to the next instruction below.

The below code uses a Do Until loop to display spot values from 1 to 5 in a dialog box. The loop terminates when the value stored in the counter variable exceeds 5.

```vba
Sub exampleDoLoopWhile()

    Dim myCounter As Integer
    myCounter = 1

    Do Until myCounter > 5
      MsgBox myCounter
      myCounter = myCounter + 1
    Loop

End Sub
```

The variations are modest, and any repetitive structure may be used. However, it is important to note that an incorrect instruction can result in an infinite loop. Therefore, it is crucial to save your code and perform all necessary checks before running it.

22.
THE "SET" STATEMENT

The SET statement enables the assignment of a snap to an object. It is particularly useful when working with Excel objects, such as cells, sheets, ranges, workbooks, or objects created in Excel. The 'set' statement establishes a connection between the variable and the memory object.

Suppose you are working with the WorkSheets(1) object in your code, you can use Range("B5") and the subsequent instructions:

- WorkSheets(1). Range("B5").value
- WorkSheets(1). Range("B5"). Font.Bold
- WorkSheets(1). Range("B5"). Font.Italic

The WorkSheets(1) object is repeated continuously, as shown by Range("B5"). To simplify the code, use "Set" to link a variable to the object.

```
Set myCell = Worksheets(1). Range("B5")
```

By using the SET statement, the code is reduced, avoiding the need to repeatedly write the same object, and saving computation time.

- myCell.value
- myCell.Font.Bold
- myCell.Font.Italic

The code example below demonstrates how programming time can be saved. To achieve this, replace the WorkSheets statement with the SET h1, SET h2, and SET h3 statements.

```vba
Option Explicit
_____

Sub myExample()
Dim h1 as Object, h2 as Object, h3 As Object
Dim matched As Integer
Dim i as Integer, j As Integer

Set h1 = Sheets("myItems")
Set h2 = Sheets("myReport")
Set h3 = Sheets("myList")

h1.Select
matched = 0

  For i = 1 To h1.Range("B" & Rows.Count).End(xlUp).Row
    For j = 1 To h2.Range("A" & Rows.Count).End(xlUp).Row
      If h1.Cells(i, "B") = h2.Cells(j, "A") Then
         matched = 1
      End If
    Next j

  If matched = 0 Then
     h1.Rows(i).EntireRow.Copy
     h3.Range ("A" & h3.Range("B" & Rows.Count).End(xlUp).Row + 1)
     matched = 0
  End If

  Next i

End Sub
```

The sheets previously named "myItem," "myList," and "myReport" have been renamed as h1, h2, and h3.

23.
ACTIVE X

ctiveX is a Microsoft technology that allows for the creation of reusable and extensible software components, known as ActiveX controls. These controls can be utilized in various applications, including Excel, Word, and Internet Explorer.

23.1. ActiveX Controls

To insert controls into your spreadsheet, activate the ActiveX control bar found in the Programmer/Developer tab → Insert option, there you will find the form controls and ActiveX controls bars.

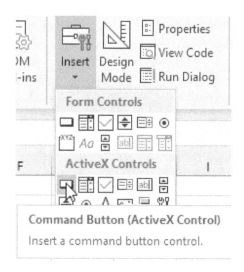

Figure 49. ActiveX controls

ActiveX controls enable the user to perform actions, such as creating a button on the same spreadsheet. When clicked, the button executes a certain code.

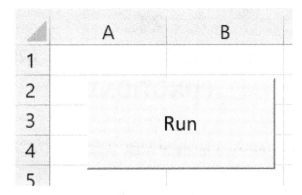

Figure 50. Adding a control button in a spreadsheet

To insert this code, double-click on the button to open the code editor associated with the button's 'Click' event. Program and save the code in the editor. When you click the button in your spreadsheet, the scheduled instructions will execute.

24.
SUB-PROGRAMS, PROCEDURES & FUNCTIONS

As is often the case in life, the 'divide and conquer' approach is commonly used in computer programming. This involves breaking down a large problem into smaller, more manageable tasks. This process is referred to as 'Top-Down design'.

This design approach promotes modularity, code reuse, and program structure clarity. Breaking down the code into smaller stages and sub-modules also facilitates collaborative development and troubleshooting, as each module can be worked on independently before being integrated into the full program. Top-down programming is a structured and systematic approach to software development that enables a gradual and modular design of the program. It starts from a high-level perspective and progresses to more detailed levels.

This programming type needs sub-programs or sub-algorithms known as procedures and **functions.**

As previously mentioned, the distinction between procedures and sub-procedures can be subtle and at times even used interchangeably. It is important to note that functions are typically referred to as procedures.

Both subprocedures and functions are blocks of code that perform specific tasks. However, there is a fundamental difference between them: Functions return a value while subprocedures (or subroutines) do not. Subprocedures can be used to manipulate data, display a message, or perform calculations without returning a value.

Functions and subprocedures may require parameters, which must be treated with a specific syntax. The syntax for handling parameters is explained below.

24.1. Parameters by ByRef reference and by ByVal value

In many cases, both subroutines and functions need to be given a list of values, called parameters, in order to find the solution to the task given to them. In a function, the parameters would be the inputs to perform some kind of calculation.

Visual Basic (VBA) has two types of parameters: ByVal parameters and ByRef references. By default, VBA works by reference, meaning that if nothing is specified, the parameter is assumed to be ByRef. However, this can be modified as needed.

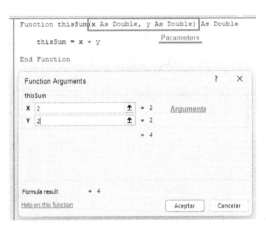

Figure 51. Parameters or arguments

A parameter passed by reference (**ByRef**) is assigned a specific memory space. This means that when the variable in the applet changes, it also changes in the main program. On the other hand, when using per-value (ByVal) parameters, any changes made in the applet do not affect the parent program.

24.2. User-Defined Roles in VBA

A function in Excel VBA is a block of code that performs a specific task and returns a value. It can have input parameters, perform calculations, or manipulate data, and finally return a result. Functions allow code to be reused in several parts of a program.

On the other hand, a function enables the creation of new functionality that is not available by default in Excel. In other words, while MS Excel has numerous functions, some may not be present. For instance, a specific function may be required to concatenate the word 'hello' with a dash and a numeric value: 'hello' & '-' & cell_value.

To create a function, first press the Alt+F11 keys (or locate it in the Visual Basic editor) and then insert a module into the worksheet.

All functions have a common syntax. The first line of code starts with the word 'function()', and the last line is 'End Function'. The code in between will always return a value, which can be of type *Double, Integer, String*, or other data types.

Function function_name (define variables, constants, etc.)

    <instructions>

function_name = return_value

End of Function

If variables are not defined, VBA will assign them a default type. Below is an example of a function that enables quick and automatic concatenation of cells, thereby enhancing the speed of creating a spreadsheet.

Option Explicit

Function concatenateCells(Range As Range)

```
For Each myCell In rango.Cells

    If myCell.value <> "" Then
        result = result & "; " & myCell.value
    End If

Next myCell

result = Right(result, Len(result) - 2)
concatenateCells = result

End Function
```

In this macro, the function name is defined as *'concatenate_cells'* after the keyword 'function'. The parameters of the function and their format are specified in parentheses. In this case, it requests a range of data in the form of an array. '.cells' represents the cells of a specified range. The "if" statement, indicates that if the cells are blank, the macro will skip them and proceed to the next statement.

Another interesting example is the multiplication of two integer values through a function.

```
Function multiplication(ByVal x As Integer, ByVal y As Integer) As Integer

    multiplication = x * y

End Function
```

A user-defined function will generate something like this:

Function Arguments   ?   ✕

multiplication

X   2   ⬆   =   2

Y   3| ⬆   =   3

=   6

Formula result   =   6

Help on this function   [Aceptar]   [Cancelar]

Figure 52. Arguments of a function

In the scenario described, it is important to declare all variables that will be used, even if there are many. To ensure this, it is recommended to use *'Option Explicit'* at the beginning of the module. After deploying the code, add a function to the icon that appears in the worksheet toolbar.

Figure 53. Selecting a User-Defined role

And then select the "User-defined" function:

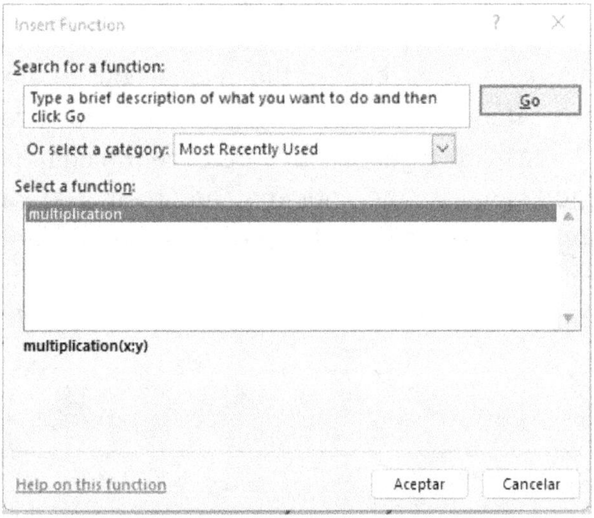

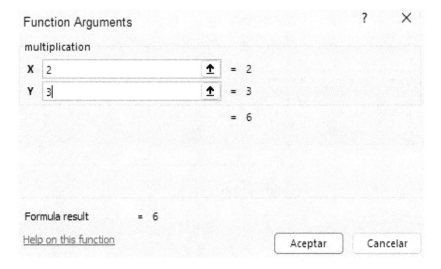

Figure 54. Inserting a function

To use the function, insert the following arguments:

Figure 55. Inserting the function arguments

24.3. ByVal and ByRef

To comprehend the dissimilarities between ByVal and byRef, it is advisable to provide an example. In VBA, ByVal is utilized to pass an argument by value, which implies that a local copy of the argument's value is generated in the function or thread. Conversely, byRef is employed to pass an argument by reference, which implies that the memory address of the original argument is passed, and modifications made within the function or subprocedure will impact the original argument. Please use the following code to your computer and observe the outcome when you execute it.

```vba
Option Explicit

Sub exampleByVal_ByRef()

    Dim a As Integer
    a = 20

    MsgBox "The original value of a is: " & a

    increaseByVal a
    MsgBox "Using ByVal the value is: " & a

    increaseByRef a
    MsgBox "Using ByRef the value is: " & a

End Sub

Sub increaseByVal(ByVal value As Integer)

    value = value + 1

End Sub

Sub increaseByRef(ByRef value As Integer)

    value = value + 1

End Sub
```

When running the code in a new module of your editor, it becomes apparent that the main program, exampleByVal_ByRef, calls two subprocedures: increaseByRef and increaseByVal. Both subprocedures are given an integer value of 20. When the increaseByVal procedure is called, a copy of the value of 'a' is passed to the subprocedure. Therefore, any changes made within the subprocedure will not affect the original value of 'a'. However, if IncreaseByRef is called, the subprocedure will directly affect the original value of 'a' since its reference is passed to the subprocedure.

Upon running the code, it becomes apparent that the value of 'a' remains unchanged after the ByVal call, whereas it is incremented by 1 after the ByRef call.

To differentiate between ByVal and ByRef values, consider the following example. Use the code below into your VBA compiler and run it:

```
Option Explicit

Sub exampleDoble()

    Dim x As Integer
    x = 10

    MsgBox x
    MsgBox myDouble(x)

End Sub


Function myDouble()

    x = x * 2
    myDouble = x

End Function
```

First, this message will appear:

And then:

Now notice what happens when you replace the ByRef with the ByVal:

And then:

25.
MULTIPLE SELECTIVE STRUCTURE

The multiple selection structure enables comparison of a value with several alternatives. If the comparison is successful, the instruction group that corresponds to the selected alternative is executed, and then the structure exits.

Multiple selective structures often have a default option that provides a solution in cases where the suggested alternatives fail.

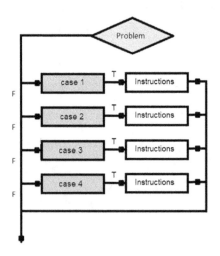

Figure 56. Multiple selective structure

```
Select case <expression>

        Case 1 Value 1
             <Instructions>
        Case 2 Value 2
             <Instructions>
        Case 3 Value 3
             <Instructions>
End Select
```

Both the 'Select Case' and the 'if' are structures used to make decisions based on certain conditions. However, the 'if' is a conditional control structure that evaluates a Boolean condition and executes a set of instructions if the condition is true. The 'Select Case' is used when evaluating a variable or expression in multiple cases, saving code and programming time. For example, try repeating the following code with an increasing number of options:

```
Sub exampleSelectCase()

Dim myOption As Integer
myOption = InputBox("Insert a value")

    Select Case myOption
        Case 1
        MsgBox "Value is one"
        Case 2
        MsgBox "Value is one"
        Case 3
        MsgBox "Value is one"
        Case 4
        MsgBox "Value is one"
        Case Else
        MsgBox "Value is out of range from 1 to 4"
    End Select
End Sub
```

26.

LOGICAL OR CHECKING FUNCTIONS

Check functions are utilized to evaluate specific variables and objects, returning a Boolean logical value (true or false). These functions also enable decision-making in code and execution of different actions based on the check results.

- IsNumeric: Verifies whether the expression has a numerical value.
- IsDate: Verifies whether the expression contains a date.
- IsEmpty: Checks to see if the expression has any data that has been initialized.
- IsError: Verifies whether the expression contains any initialized data.
- IsArray: Verifies if the variable is an array.
- isObject: Verifies whether a variable represents an object.
- IsNull: Checks whether the expression contains a null value due to invalid data.
- IsEmpty: Verifies whether any cells or ranges are empty or contain outdated information.
- Is Nothing: Verifies the existence of an object.

To comprehend the utility of check functions, consider the following example: declare a variable as an object and assign it any object. If such an object exists, a pop-up sale will report it. Conversely, if the object is 'Nothing', it indicates that the variable does not exist.

```
Sub checkIsNothing()

Dim myVariable As Object
Set myVariable = Worksheets("sheet1").Range("A1").Value
'Set myVariable = Nothing

        If myVariable Is Nothing Then
            MsgBox "The variable is empty"
                Else
                    MsgBox "The variable is not empty"
            End if
End Sub
```

This example checks if cell 'A1' contains any values and displays a message in a dialog box indicating if it is empty.

```
Sub checkIsEmpty()

        If IsEmpty(Worksheets("sheet1").Range("A1").Value) Then
            MsgBox "The variable is empty"
                Else
                    MsgBox "The variable is not empty"
            End if
End Sub
```

Another benefit of these features is that they enable quick decision-making within the code without the need for more complex forms of coding.

27.
THE INTERSECT INSTRUCTION

The 'intersect' statement in VBA for Excel is utilized to determine the intersection between two or more cell ranges. The syntax is as follows:

Set myIntersect = intersect(rank1, rank2, ..., rankN)

The 'intersect' statement returns a range object that represents the intersection between two given ranges. If the ranges do not intersect, the function returns 'nothing'.

The intersect function is helpful for performing conditional or manipulative operations on cells that are at the intersection of two or more specific ranges.

In the following code, the message 'hello' appears when the active cell is placed above A1, and 'no' appears in any other cell.

```
Option explicit


Sub hello()

        If not Intersect(ActiveCell, Range("A1")) Is Nothing Then
                MsgBox "Hello"
                    Else
                        MsgBox "NO"
            End If
End Sub
```

Consider another example where Range1 is defined as cells A1 through B6 and Range2 as cells B4 through C8. Then, to check if there is an intersection between the two ranges, use the 'intersect' function. If there is an intersection, a message will be displayed in a window indicating that it does not exist.

```vba
Option Explicit


Sub checkIntersection()

Dim range1 As Range
Dim range2 As Range
Dim rangeIntersection As Range

Set range1 = Range("A1:B6")
Set range2 = Range("B4:C8")
Set rangeIntersection = Intersect (range1, range2)

            If not rangeIntersection Is Nothing Then
                MsgBox "There are an intersection between them"
                        Else
                            MsgBox "There are NOT an intersection between
them"
                End If
End Sub
```

28.
SOLVED EXAMPLES

This book contains a series of exercises solved in Visual Basic, with a focus on Excel. Although the book is oriented towards Microsoft spreadsheets, it is still useful to know because Visual Basic is a valuable language for .NET technology.

The aim is for the reader to feel included in the community of developers and to enable them to begin working in other programming languages.

Furthermore, the following exercises aid in the comprehension of and improving the concepts. The exercises focus on:

- Imperative Programming
- Conditionals, "if", "Select Case", "Chose" and "Switch"
- Loops for, while, do and for Each
- Functions, procedures, and sub-algorithms
- Graphics
- Multimedia
- Classes & Objects
- Macro Recording
- Events
- Skills
- Error Handling
- Concepts. Build policies
- Variables, Constants, and Types
- Collections & Arrays
- Concepts. The Nested With
- Concepts. Build policies
- Concepts: GoSub
- Concepts: On... GoSub

144

- Concepts: Wilds and the "like" operator
- Concepts: The Nothing
- Concepts. Random
- Concepts. Time and dates
- Concepts. The Assert
- Concepts. The Stop
- Concepts. Name shading
- Concepts. Parameterized Procedures

28.1. Exercise number 01

Type: Imperative programming.

Problem: Perform an addition operation using two integers' numbers.

Solution: To solve this problem, create a UserForm that prompts the user to input two integer values. The result will be displayed after the user presses a button.

1. First, create the UserForms as shown below:

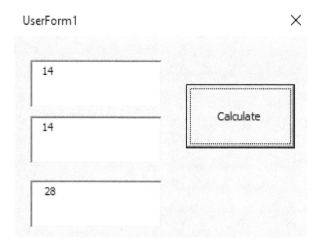

Figure 57. Sum of two integers

2. Type the provided code after double-clicking on the calculate button.

```vba
Option Explicit
```

```vba
Private Sub CommandButton1_Click()

        'Declare variables
        Dim A As Integer
        Dim B As Integer
        Dim C As Integer

        'Entries
        A = Val(Me.TextBox1.Text) 'Pass the data of the InputBox to a
numeric value
        B = Val(Me.TextBox2.Text) 'Pass the data of the InputBox to a
numeric value

        'Outputs
        C = A + B 'Perform the sum
        Me.TextBox3.Text = Str(C)

End Sub
```

28.2. Exercise number 02

Type: Imperative programming.

Problem: Calculate the quotient and remainder resulting from the division of any two numbers.

Solution: To find the quotient and the remainder, create a table as in the previous exercise where in a UserForm, the values are entered, and the result is displayed.

3. First, create the UserForms as shown below:

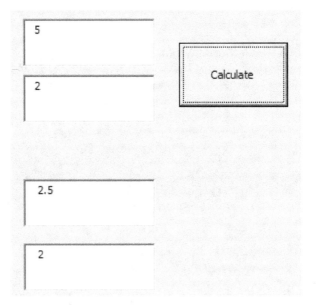

Figure 58. Quotient and remainder of a division of numbers

4. Type the provided code after double-clicking on the calculate button.

```vb
Private Sub CommandButton1_Click()
    ' Declare variables
    Dim A As Double
    Dim B As Double
    Dim C As Double

    'Inputs
    A = Val(Me.TextBox1.Text) 'Pass the data of the InputBox to a numeric
value.
    B = Val(Me.TextBox2.Text) 'Pass the data of the InputBox to a numeric
value.

    'Outputs
    C = A / B 'Perform the division
    Me.TextBox3.Text = Str(C)

    ' Pass the data in the table to a numerical value
    D = A \ B  ' Do the remainder
    Me.TextBox4.Text = Str(D)
End Sub
```

28.3. Exercise number 03

Type: Imperative programming.

Problem: Calculate the percentage of a value and display its result.

Solution: To calculate the percentage of a value, create a UserForm that requests two values and displays the product as the result.

5. First, create the UserForms as shown below:

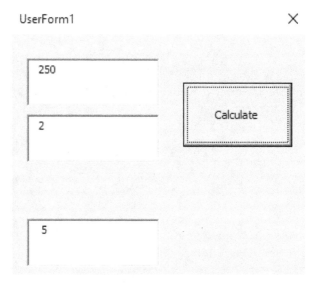

Figure 59. Percentage of a value

6. Type the provided code after double-clicking on the calculate button.

```
Private Sub CommandButton1_Click()
   ' Declare variables
   Dim A As Double 'Value A
   Dim B As Double ' Ratio percent
   Dim C As Double  ' Result

   'Inputs
   A = Val(Me.TextBox1.Text) 'Pass the data of the InputBox to a numeric
value.
   B = Val(Me.TextBox2.Text)  'Pass the data of the InputBox to a numeric
value.

   'Outputs
   C = A * B / 100 'Perform the operation
   Me.TextBox3.Text = Str(C)

End Sub
```

28.4. Exercise number 04

Type: Imperative programming.

Problem: Raise a number to another number, from A to the power of B.

Solution: To calculate the power of a value, create a UserForm that requests two values, performs the calculation, and displays the result later.

1. First, make the following chart with the UserForms:

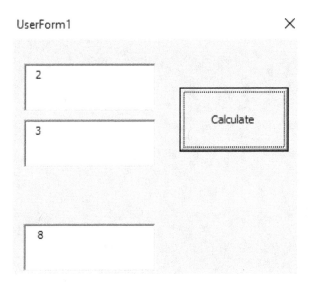

Figure 60. Exponent from one number to another

2. Type the provided code after double-clicking on the calculate button.

```
Private Sub CommandButton1_Click()
   ' Declare variables
   Dim A As Double 'Base
   Dim B As Double 'Exponent
   Dim C As Double  'Result

   'Inputs
   A = Val(Me.TextBox1.Text) 'Pass the data of the InputBox to a numeric
value.
   B = Val(Me.TextBox2.Text)  'Pass the data of the InputBox to a numeric
value.

   'Outputs
   C = A ^ B  'Perform the operation
   Me.TextBox3.Text = Str(C)
End Sub
```

28.5. Exercise number 05

Type: Imperative programming.

Problem: Type a text into the text box and click a button to display it backwards. For example, ABCDEF becomes FEDCBA.

Solution: To solve the problem, create a UserForm that requests a text and then displays it inverted.

3. First, make the following chart with the UserForms:

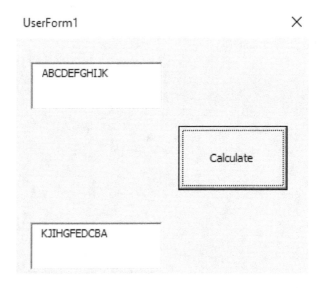

Figure 61. Character Inversion

4. Type the provided code after double-clicking on the calculate button.

```vba
Private Sub CommandButton1_Click()
  ' Declare variables
  Dim A As String 'Input Text
  Dim B As String 'Result

  'Inputs
  A = Me.TextBox1.Text 'Catch the text

  'Outputs
  B = StrReverse (A) 'Perform the inversion
  Me.TextBox3.Text = Str(B)

End Sub
```

Note: In this example, we used a VBA function called StrReverse() to reverse the direction of the text.

28.6. Exercise number 06

Type: Imperative Programming

Problem: Find the hypotenuse of a triangle using the Pythagorean theorem. $h^2 = a^2 + b^2$.

Solution: To perform this calculation, it is necessary to know that the hypotenuse can be calculated using the formula: $h = \sqrt{(a^2 + b^2)}$. The symbol √ represents the square root, which is equivalent to raising the sum of the squares to the power of 1/2.

1. Firstly, create a UserForm with two text boxes named textBox1 and textBox2, representing variables "a" and "b" respectively. The result should be displayed in TextBox3.

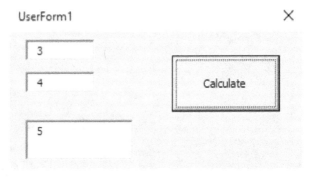

Figure 62. Hypotenuse of a right triangle

2. Above the 'calculate' button, type the following code after double-clicking on it:

```
Private Sub CommandButton1_Click()
  ' Declare variables
  Dim A As Double
  Dim B As Double

  'Inputs
  A = Me.TextBox1.Text
  B = Me.TextBox2.Text

  'Outputs
  Me.TextBox3.Text = Sqr((A ^ 2) + (B ^ 2))
End Sub
```

28.7. Exercise number 07

Type: Imperative Programming

Problem: Perform a UserForm to input two values, then add them together, and display the result in a cell.

Solution: This exercise is useful for creating forms on an Excel page.

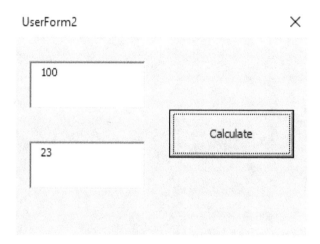

Figure 63. Sum of two values

To perform the exercise, use the following code:

```
Private Sub CommandButton1_Click()

    ' Declare variables
    Dim val1 As Double
    Dim val2 As Double

    'Inputs
    Val1 = Me.TextBox1.Text  'Pass the data of the InputBox to a numeric value.
    Val2 = Me.TextBox2.Text  'Pass the data of the InputBox to a numeric value.

    'Outputs
    Range("A1").Value = val1 + val2

End Sub
```

Note: A UserForm could be useful, for instance, if you needed to create an Excel invoice that calculates the total cost of a customer's purchases while accounting for real estate taxes.

28.8. Exercise number 08

Type: Imperative Programming

Problem: Given a sentence, return the encrypted phrase using the Caesar code method.

Solution: The Caesar code is a well-studied cryptographic method that involves reassigning each letter of the alphabet to a different one by shifting a specific number of positions. This simple and useful method has made the Caesar code a popular topic in cryptography. Stanley Kubrick's 2001: A Space Odyssey showcases the HAL 9000 supercomputer, named by shifting each letter of the famous computer brand IBM one position. Thus, the equation A + 1 position = B holds true. Afterwards, generate a UserForm where you can input the desired phrase and the number of letters to be processed.

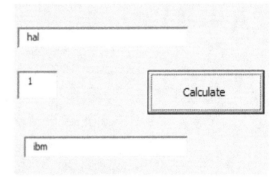

Figure 64. Caesar code

The code could look like this:

```
Private Sub calcule_Click()

Dim a, b, c As String
Dim d, i As Integer

a = Me.TextBox1.Text
d = CInt(Me.TextBox2.Text)
a = Trim(a)

For i = 1 To Len(a)

    c = Mid(a, i, 1)

    If c <> "" Then
        c = Chr(Asc(c) + d)
    End If
    b = b & c

Next

Me.TextBox3.Text = b
End Sub
```

28.9. Exercise number 09

Type: Conditionals, "if", "Select Case", "Chose" and "Switch"

Problem: Given two different numbers find a return the lesser of both values.

Solution: To determine the smaller value between two given values, create a UserForm that prompts the user to input the values and then displays the smaller result.

1. First, make the following chart with the UserForms:

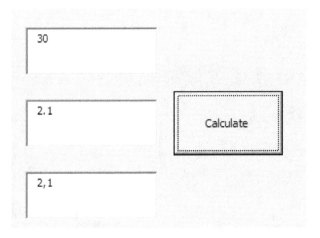

Figure 65. Finding the lower value between two

2. Above the 'calculate' button, add the following code after double-clicking on the created UserForm:

```
Private Sub CommandButton1_Click ( )

' Declare variables
Dim A As Double 'First Input text
Dim B As Double 'Second Input text

' Inputs
A = Val (Me. TextBox1.Text)
B = Val (Me. TextBox2.Text)

' Outputs
        If A < B Then
                Me. TextBox3.Text = A
        Else
                Me. TextBox3.Text = B
        End If

        If A = B Then
                Me. TextBox3. Text = "Both are equal"
        End If
End Sub
```

28.10. Exercise number 10

Type: Conditionals, "if", "Select Case", "Chose" and "Switch"

Problem: Given a character, analyze whether it is a consonant or a vowel.

Solution: To determine whether a character is a vowel or a consonant, create a UserForm that requests a piece of data and then displays the result as either 'VOWEL' or 'CONSONANT'.

1. First, make the following chart with the UserForms:

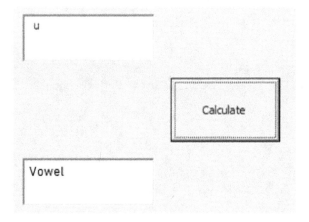

Figure 66. Recognize vowels or consonants

2. By double-clicking on the created UserForm, place the following code, specifically above the "calculate" button:

```
Private Sub Calculate_Click()
' Declare variables
Dim Entry As String 'String Input
'Input
Entry = Me.TextBox1.Text
' Outputs
   If Entry = "a" Or Entry = "A" Then
      Me.TextBox2.Text = "Vowel"
         ElseIf Entry = "e" Or Entry = "E" Then
            Me.TextBox2.Text = " Vowel "
               ElseIf Entry = "i" Or Entry = "I" Then
                  Me.TextBox2.Text = " Vowel "
                     ElseIf Entry = "o" Or Entry = "O" Then
                        Me.TextBox2.Text = " Vowel "
                           ElseIf Entry = "u" Or Entry = "U" Then
                              Me.TextBox2.Text = " Vowel "
                           Else
                              Me.TextBox2.Text = "Consonant"
   End If
End Sub
```

28.11. Exercise number 11

Type: Conditionals, "if", "Select Case", "Chose" and "Switch"

Problem: Given an integer value, get the decomposition of a value into prime numbers.

Solution: To analyze what the decomposition of a value is into prime numbers, create a UserForms, where a piece of data is requested and then the result is displayed:

3. First, make the following chart with the UserForms:

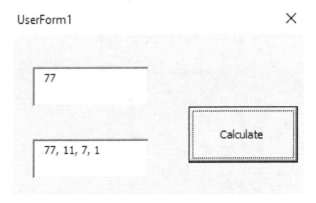

Figure 67. Decomposition into prime numbers

4. By double-clicking on the created UserForm, type the following code, specifically above the "calculate" button:

```
Option Explicit
_____

Private Sub Calculate_Click()
    Dim num As Integer
    Dim i As Integer
    Dim result As String
        num = Val(Me.TextBox1.Text)
        For i = 1 To num
            If (num Mod i) = 0 Then
                result = CStr(i) & "," & result
                    Me.TextBox2.Text = result
            End If
        Next
End Sub
```

Note: In this problem, the 'for' loop iterates through all values from 1 to the number entered in the text field. The 'if' statement checks if the remainder (mod) is zero. If it is, the old result is concatenated with the new one and displayed in the dialog box. This exercise is more complex than the previous ones but is still interesting. It is worth noting that it is common to use the 'if' and 'for' statements together.

28.12. Exercise number 12

Type: Conditionals, "if", "Select Case", "Chose" and "Switch"

Problem: Given an integer value result in the following table names:
1. Andorra, 2. Scotland, 3. Latvia, 4. Catalonia, 5. Italy.

Solution: To display the result according to the above classification, create a UserForms, where a value is requested and then the result is displayed:

5. First, make the following chart with the UserForms:

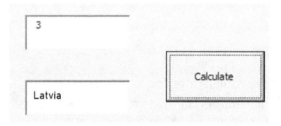

Figure 68. Example of "Select Case"

6. By double-clicking on the created UserForm, insert the following code, specifically above the "calculate" button:

```
Option Explicit
_____

Private Sub Calculate_Click()

Dim num As Integer
Dim result As String
num = Val(Me.TextBox1.Text)

Select Case num 'Map integer value to country name

        Case 1
        result = "Andorra"
        Case 2
        result = " Scotland "
        Case 3
        result = "Latvia"
        Case 4
        result = "Catalonia"
        Case 5
        result = "Italia"
        Case Is > 5
        result = "Other"
        Case Is < 1
        result = "Other"
   End Select

Me.TextBox2.Text = result
End Sub
```

Note: The problem presented is interesting as it utilizes the 'Select Case' method to analyze whether a number is greater or lesser than a specific value.

28.13. Exercise number 13

Type: Conditionals, "if", "Select Case", "Chose" and "Switch"

Problem: Given the following table displays whether a person is classified as tall, medium, or short after entering the height in centimeters and body type.

	High	Medium	Low
Woman	180	170	160
Man	190	180	170
Child	100	90	80

Table 12. Person's height rating

Solution: To display the results as per the table, create a UserForm. Select the gender and status, and then provide the height in centimeters before pressing the calculate button.

7. First, make the following chart with the UserForms:

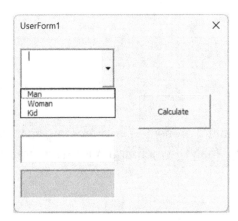

Figure 69. Example of conditionals

8. By double-clicking on the created UserForm, insert the following code, specifically above the "calculate" button:

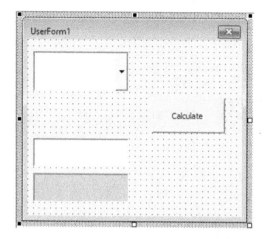

Figure 70. Modelling a userForm

```
Option Explicit
_____

Private Sub calculate_Click()
Dim num As Integer
Dim mySelection As Integer

num = Val(Me.textbox1.Text)
mySelection = Me.comboBox1.ListIndex

  Select Case mySelection

    Case 0

        If num >= 180 Then
        Me.textbox2.Text = "Tall"
        ElseIf 180 > num <= 170 Then
        Me.textbox2.Text = "Medium"
        ElseIf 160 >= num Then
        Me.textbox2.Text = "Short"
        End If

    Case 1
        If num >= 190 Then
        Me.textbox2.Text = "Tall"
        ElseIf 190 > num <= 180 Then
        Me.textbox2.Text = "Medium"
        ElseIf 170 >= num Then
        Me.textbox2.Text = "Short"
```

```
            End If

        Case 2
          If num >= 100 Then
          Me.textbox2.Text = "Tall"
          ElseIf 100 > num <= 90 Then
          Me.textbox2.Text = "Medium"
          ElseIf 90 >= num Then
          Me.textbox2.Text = "Short"
          End If
        End Select
      End Sub
```

```
Private Sub UserForm_Initialize()
  comboBox1.AddItem "Man"
  comboBox1.AddItem "Woman"
  comboBox1.AddItem "Kid"
End Sub
```

28.14. Exercise number 14

Type: Conditionals, "if", "Select Case", "Chose" and "Switch"

Problem: Convert a Roman numeral to the decimal (Indo-Arabic) numeral system.

Solution: The exercise does not address more complex issues, such as roman number cases IX or IV. The problem is presented in a simple manner. Enter a letter in either uppercase or lowercase and click the calculate button to display the result in the second text box.

1. First make the following box with the UserForms:

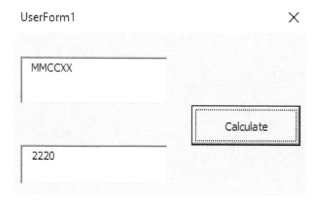

Figure 71. Converting a roman number to a decimal number

2.Double-click on the created UserForm and insert the following code on the "calculate" button:

Option Explicit

```
Private Sub Calculate_Click()
  Dim romanNumber As String
  Dim a As String
  Dim num As Integer
  Dim result As Integer
  Dim z As Integer
  romanNumber = Me.TextBox1.Text
    For z = 1 To Len(romanNumber)
      a = Mid(romanNumber, z, 1)

      Select Case a
        Case "I", "i"
        num = 1
        Case "V", "v"
        num = 5
        Case "X", "x"
        num = 10
        Case "L", "l"
        num = 50
        Case "C", "c"
        num = 100
        Case "D", "d"
        num = 500
        Case "M", "m"
        num = 1000
        Case "G", "g"
        num = 5000
      End Select
      result = num + result

      Me.TextBox2.Text = result
    Next z
End Sub
```

Note: If you wish, you could try the above exercise and then consider the problem of what a number like IX, which is not equal to 11, would look like in Roman numerals. It is important to note that MS Excel has its own functions for converting Roman numerals to decimals and vice versa.

28.15. Exercise number 15

Type: Conditionals, "if", "Select Case", "Chose" and "Switch"

Problem: Color odd numbers in a column of data green.

Solution: To achieve this, the program must iterate through all the cells in a data column and paint the cells green if the data is odd. Use the following code to accomplish this:

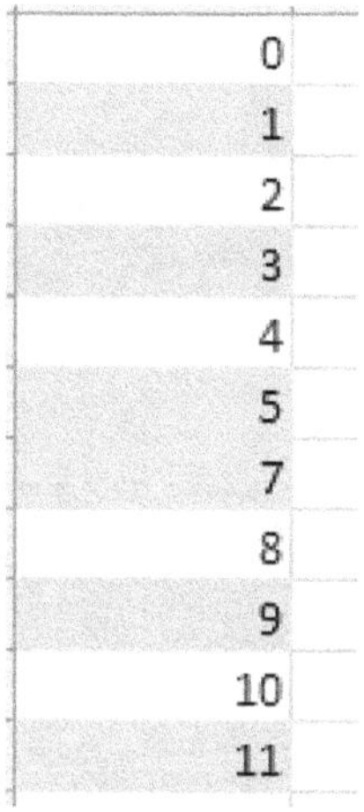

0
1
2
3
4
5
7
8
9
10
11

Figure 72. Example of coloring cells using conditionals

In this case, the code colors the data in column "A":

```
Option Explicit
```

```
Sub colouringCells()

Dim i As Integer
Dim num As Double

  For i = 1 To Range("A" & Rows.Count).End(xlUp)
    Cells(i, 1).Interior.ColorIndex = 0  'Firstly, remove any previous colors
from the cells
      num = Cells(i, 1).Value
    If num Mod 2 <> 0 Then
      Cells(i, 1).Interior.ColorIndex = 4 'Coloring green the non-even cells
    End If

Next i
End Sub
```

28.16. Exercise number 16

Type: Conditionals, "if", "Select Case", "Chose" and "Switch"

Problem: Perform the game of "rock, paper, scissors." The user will be prompted to select either rock, paper, or scissors. The computer will randomly select one of the options, and the outcome will be determined as either a win or a tie.

Solution: Create an InputBox where you can write the option: rock, paper, or scissors:

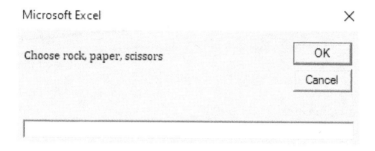

Figure 73. Game of rock, paper, scissors

You can then use the following code:

```vba
Option Explicit
```

```vba
Sub gameStonePaperScissors()

    Dim chooseGamer As String
    Dim chooseComputer As String
    Dim winner As String

    'Ask to the user choose between paper, scissors o stone
    chooseGamer = LCase(InputBox("Choose Stone, Paper or Scissors."))

    'Generates a choice randomly for the player-computer
    Select Case Int(Rnd * 3)
        Case 0
        chooseComputer = "Stone"
        Case 1
        chooseComputer = "Paper"
        Case 2
        chooseComputer = "Scissors"
    End Select

        'Code which choose the winner
        If chooseGamer = "stone" And chooseComputer = "Scissors" Or _
            chooseGamer = "paper" And chooseComputer = "stone" Or _
            chooseGamer = "scissors" And chooseComputer = "paper" Then
        winner = "Gamer"

        ElseIf chooseGamer = "Scissors" And chooseComputer = "Stone" Or _
        chooseGamer = "Stone" And chooseComputer = "paper" Or _
        chooseGamer = "paper" And chooseComputer = "Scissors" Then
        winner = "Computer"

        Else
        winner = "draw"

    End If

    MsgBox "The player choose: " & chooseGamer & "." & vbCrLf & _
    "The computer choose: " & chooseComputer & "." & vbCrLf & vbCrLf & _
    "The winner is: " & winner & "!"

End Sub
```

28.17. Exercise number 17

Type: Conditionals, "if", "Select Case", "Chose" and "Switch"

Problem: Create a VBA procedure named *'selectCase0'* that utilizes a string variable *'myText'* to display a message in a dialog box based on the different possible values of the string 'myText'. If 'myText' contains the values 'one', 'two' or 'three', the message 'Hello!' will be displayed. If it contains the values 'five', 'six', or 'seven', the message 'Goodbye' will be displayed. Otherwise, the message 'It is not my number' will be displayed. The procedure should use a Select Case statement.

Solution: Several examples of the 'Select Case' have been presented in this work. However, we have not yet analyzed a configuration that allows us to combine the different options of each case with a comma, using the same logic as the logical operator 'O'.

```
Option Explicit


Public Sub exampleSelectCase()
Dim myText As String
myText = "one"

   Select Case myText
      Case "one", "two", "three"
      MsgBox "Hello!"
      Case "five", "six", "seven"
      MsgBox "Goodbye!"
      Case Else
      MsgBox "It is not my number

   End Select
End Sub
```

The 'Select Case' statement compares the 'hello' text with the different options of each case. If 'hello' matches one of the three options per case, then that case is executed.

Figure 74. Dialog box from the "Select Case"

28.18. Exercise number 18

Type: Conditionals, "if", "Select Case", "Chose" and "Switch"

Problem: Create an Excel spreadsheet with numerical data in column A. In column B, display the word 'greater' if the cell value in column A is greater than 10, and *"smaller"* if the cell value in column A is less than or equal to 10. To accomplish this, utilize the IIf (Inline If) function.

	A	B
1	19	greater than
2	13	greater than
3	48	greater than
4	8	smaller than
5	23	greater than
6	12	greater than

Figure 75. Example of IIf (Inline If)

Solution:

- Use the variable "i" to cycle through all the rows with data in column A.
- The For loop starts in row 1 and ends in the last row with data from column A (obtained using the Range("A" & Rows.Count statement). End(xlUp). Row).
- Within the loop, the IIf function is used to evaluate whether the value in column A is greater than 10. If true, write "major" in column B; otherwise, it is written "minor".
- The result of the IIf function is assigned to the corresponding cell in column B using Range("B" & i). Value.

```
Option Explicit
```

```
Sub example_IIf()
    Dim i As Integer
    For i = 1 To Range("A" & Rows.Count).End(xlUp).Row
        Range("B" & i).Value = IIf(Range("A" & i).Value > 10, "greater",
"minor")
    Next i
End Sub
```

The solution described could have been implemented using traditional construction with *if... elseif... else...* statements. However, the IIf (Inline If) function is a quicker alternative that evaluates an expression and returns a value based on its truthfulness. This function is used to avoid the need for an If statement. The *Then... Else* statement is used when a simple assessment is required. Simply knowing the expression to be evaluated and the appropriate actions for true or false results is sufficient. Its syntax is as follows:

```
IIf(expression, true_valor, false_value)
```

28.19. Exercise number 19

Type: Conditionals, "if", "Select Case", "Chose" and "Switch"

Problem: Create a column B in an Excel spreadsheet that displays a text string based on the value in column A, follow these steps: use the 'Switch' function and set the conditions for each value. If the value in column A is less than zero, the function will return 'negative'. If the value is greater than or equal to zero, it will return 'positive'. If the value is null, it will return 'zero'.

	A	B
1	-6	Negative
2	9	Positive
3	-10	Negative
4	-6	Negative
5	-7	Negative
6	6	Positive

Figure 76. Example of "Switch"

Solution: The Switch function is a conditional function that evaluates multiple conditions and returns a value corresponding to the first case that is met. The function is used to avoid having to write an If declaration. Then... Else completes when only multiple assessment is required. Its syntax is as follows:

Switch(expression1, value1, expression2, value2, ..., expressionN, Nvalue, predetermined_value)

- expression1, expression2, ..., expression are evaluations that return true or false.
- value1, value2, ..., valueN are the values that will be returned if the corresponding expressions are true.
- predetermined_value is the value that will be returned if none of the expressions are true.

With all these concepts clear, the problem can be solved as follows:

- Use the variable "i" to cycle through all the rows with data in column A.
- The "For" loop starts in row 1 and ends in the last row with data in column A (obtained with Range("A" & Rows.Count). End(xlUp). Row).
- Within the loop, the Switch function is used to evaluate the value in column A and return a corresponding text string.
- The Switch function evaluates each of the provided conditions and returns the corresponding value of the first case that is met. If the value in column A is less than 0, 'Negative' is returned. If it is equal to 0, 'Zero' is returned. If it is greater than 0, 'Positive' is returned.
- The output of the Switch function is assigned to the corresponding cell in column B using the Range("B" & i statement). Value.

```
Option Explicit


Sub example_Switch()
Dim i As Integer

  For i = 1 To Range("A" & Rows.Count).End(xlUp).Row
    Range("B" & i).Value = Switch(Range("A" & i).Value < 0, "Negative", _
    Range("A" & i).Value = 0, "Zero", Range("A" & i).Value > 0, "Positive")
  Next i

End Sub
```

28.20. Exercise number 20

Type: Conditionals, "if", "Select Case", "Chose" and "Switch"

Problem: Enter a number from 1 to 3 in an InputBox and use the *Choose* function to return the same number entered in String format. If the number is different from 1 and 3, the program will display a message indicating that the data entered is not correct.

Solution: The Choose function in Excel's VBA is a useful tool for selecting a value from a list of values based on a numeric index. Its syntax is as follows:

Choose(index, case1, case2, ..., case29)

Where:

- Index is an integer that indicates the position of the value you wish to select. It must be a number between 1 and the total number of values in the list.
- Case1, Case2, ..., Case29: These are the possible values that can be selected.

The *Choose* function returns the value that corresponds to the specified index. For instance, if the index is 2, the *Choose function* returns the value of case2. A code to solve the problem would be:

Option Explicit

```vba
Sub ExampleChooseFunction()
    Dim selectedNumber As Integer
    'The user is prompted to select a number between 1 and 3.
    selectedNumber = InputBox("Chose a number between 1 to 3")

    If selectedNumber >= 1 And selectedNumber <= 3 Then
        'The Choose function is utilized to generate a result based on the user's selection.
        MsgBox Choose(selectedNumber, "One", "Two", "Three")
    Else
        'If the selected number is outside the valid range of values, an error message will be_ displayed.
        MsgBox "The chosen number is outside the valid range of values."
    End If
End Sub
```

28.21. Exercise number 21

Type: Loops for, while, do, and for Each.

Problem: Given multiple numbers, return a list in descending order and sort the numbers that exist within the range.

Solution: To display a range of sorted numbers, create a UserForm with a text box and a calculate button. Select the data and click after the calculate button.

First, make the following chart with the UserForms:

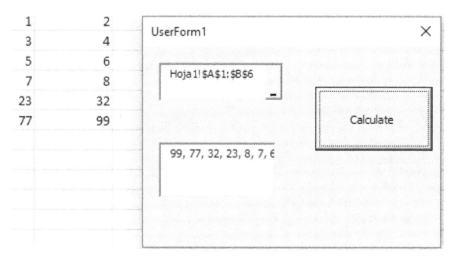

Figure 77. Example of sorting according to a criterion

To add the necessary code, double-click on the 'calculate' button of the UserForm. Then, input the following instructions:

```vba
Option Explicit
```

```vba
Private Sub Calculate_Click()
Dim j As Long
Dim i As Long
Dim temporal As Double
Dim myRange As Range
Dim result As String

  Set myRange = Range(RefEdit1.Value)   'Selection


  For i = 1 To myRange.Cells.Count
    For j = 1 To myRange.Cells.Count
      If myRange.Cells(i).Value < myRange.Cells(j).Value Then

        temporal = myRange.Cells(i).Value
        myRange.Cells(i).Value = myRange.Cells(j).Value
        myRange.Cells(j).Value = temporal

      End If
    Next j
  Next i

  For i = 1 To myRange.Cells.Count
    result = CStr(myRange.Cells(i).Value) & ", " & result
    Me.TextBox1.Text = result
  Next
End Sub
```

28.22. Exercise number 22

Type: Loops for, while, do and for each.

Problem: Use Simpson's first rule to calculate the area by knowing three ordinates of a semicircle with radius R = 6.

Solution: This problem is interesting because it enables the calculation of a figure's area through a simple numerical method, using only equally spaced ordinates. In other words, the geometric properties of a figure can be determined by measuring a certain number of heights from the base of the figure to its profile.

The statement indicates that Simpson's first rule should be used, which involves using the following expression.

$$I = \frac{h}{3} \cdot (1 \cdot y_1 + 4 \cdot y_2 + 2 \cdot y_3 + 4 \cdot y_4 + 2 \cdot y_5 + 4 \cdot y_6 + \cdots + 2 \cdot y_{n-2} + 4 \cdot y_{n-1} + 1 \cdot y_n)$$

Where the "y" is the ordinate (the height) equally spaced a constant interval "h". The formula is headed by the letter "I" for integration. Integration or integrate, in short, means to add. Although the mathematical proof of the method is complex, it has enormous potential for calculations involving integrals and derivatives. The method involves integrating equally spaced areas to calculate volume.

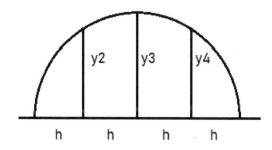

Figure 78. Calculating areas with Simpson's first rule

y_x	Factor Simpson	Factor Area
0	1	0
5,196	4	20,784
6	2	12
5,196	4	20,784
0	1	0
	Total	53,568
	Semicircle Area	53,568

Table 13. Simpson factors for area calculation

What has been achieved is the following product, knowing that h = 3:

$$A \approx \frac{3}{3} \cdot (1 \cdot 0 + 4 \cdot 5{,}196 + 2 \cdot 6 + 4 \cdot 5{,}196 + 1 \cdot 0) = 53{,}568$$

The error made is 5% with only using few ordinates and knowing that $A_{semicircle} = \pi \cdot R^2 /2 = 56.5486678$. The error decreases as the number of ordinates increases. This method is useful for calculating a ship's waterfront centers, area and inertia moments, etc. Other numerical methods, such as Simpson's second rule, can also achieve the same result.

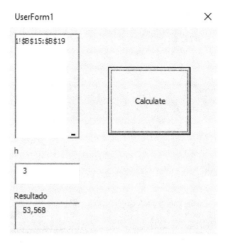

Figure 79. UserForm with first Simpson's rule

To solve the exercise, create a UserForm with a refEdit to select the data. Then, enter the space between the 'h' ordinates in one textBox and the result will be displayed in another textBox after clicking the 'calculate' button. Use the following code:

```
Option Explicit
```

```
Private Sub CommandButton1_Click()

Dim rango As Range
Dim myRange As Range
Dim evenFS As Double
Dim oddFS As Double
Dim extremFS As Double
Dim total As Double
Dim i As Integer

Set myRange = Range(refEdit1.Value)

   If (myRange.Cells.Count Mod 2) = 0 Then 'Firstly, check that rule is
adequate
      MsgBox "The first rule of Simpson only can be applied on odd ordinate"
         ElseIf (myRange.Cells.Count Mod 2) <> 0 Then 'if the number of data is
odd, then pursue

            For i = 1 To myRange.Cells.Count
               If i = 1 Or i = myRange.Cells.Count Then 'at the extremes it is
multiplied by one
                  extremFS = extremFS + 1 * myRange.Cells(i).Value
                     ElseIf (i Mod 2) = 0 Then 'for the odd item it is multiplied by
four
                        evenFS = evenFS + 4 * myRange.Cells(i).Value
                           ElseIf (i Mod 2) <> 0 Then 'for the odd item it is multiplied
by two
                              oddFS = oddFS + 2 * myRange.Cells(i).Value
               End If
            Next i

   'display result
   Me.textbox2.Text = CStr(Val(Me.textbox1.Text) * (1 / 3) * (extremFS +
oddFS + evenFS))

End If

End Sub
```

28.23. Exercise number 23

Type: Loops for, while, do and for each.

Problem: Calculate areas or volumes using Simpson's first and second rules.

Solution: The previous section discussed Simpson's first rule and its limitation to numbers of ordinates. To cover all cases, a code that includes both the first and second Simpson's rules is needed. Simpson's second rule is as follows:

$$I = \frac{3 \cdot h}{8} \cdot (1 \cdot y_1 + 3 \cdot y_2 + 3 \cdot y_3 + 2 \cdot y_4 + 3 \cdot y_5 + 3 \cdot y_6 + 2 \cdot y_7 + \cdots$$
$$\cdots + 2 \cdot y_{n-3} + 3 \cdot y_{n-2} + 3 \cdot y_{n-1} + 1 \cdot y_n)$$

The Simpson's rule, named after the British mathematician Thomas Simpson, was first introduced by Evangelista Torricelli. It corresponds to a rule that Johannes Kepler had expounded in 1615. Kepler observed a winemaker calculating the wine from some barrels using a yardstick, which inspired him to develop this method. However, he believed that the accuracy of the method was not very reliable. In 1615, he wrote the work entitled *Stereometria doliorum vinariorum*. In this work, the author explains a more precise method for calculating the quantity of wine per barrel, using parables that have been known since Archimedes.

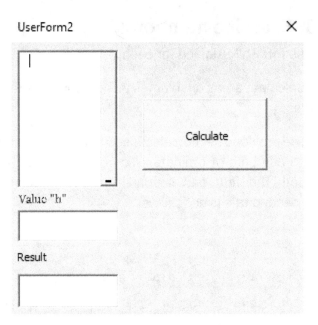

Figure 80. UserForm for Simpson's rules

```vba
Private Sub CommandButton1_Click()

Dim rango As Range
Dim myRange As Range
Dim evenFS As Double
Dim oddFS As Double
Dim extremFS As Double
Dim falseFS As Double, trueFS As Double
Dim a, total As Double
Dim i As Integer

Set myRange = Range(RefEdit1.Value)

    If (myRange.Cells.Count Mod 2) = 0 Then 'Firstly, check that rule is
adequate
        For i = 1 To myRange.Cells.Count
        a = (i - 4) / 3 'calculation to analyze when we have to use FS = 2
            If i = 1 Or i = myRange.Cells.Count Then
                extremFS = extremFS + 1 * myRange.Cells(i).Value
                ElseIf i > 1 And a <> Int(a) Then 'analyze is in an integer o no
                    falseFS = falseFS + 3 * myRange.Cells(i).Value 'if "a" is not an
integer multiply by 3.
                    ElseIf a = Int(a) And i < myRange.Cells.Count Then
                        trueFS = trueFS + 2 * myRange.Cells(i).Value 'if "a" is not
an integer multiply by 2.
                End If
        Next i

    'display result
    Me.TextBox1.Text = CStr(Val(Me.TextBox2.Text) * (3 / 8) * (extremFS +
falseFS + trueFS))

    Else
        For i = 1 To myRange.Cells.Count
        If i = 1 Or i = myRange.Cells.Count Then
            extremFS = extremFS + 1 * myRange.Cells(i).Value
            ElseIf (i Mod 2) = 0 Then
                evenFS = evenFS + 4 * myRange.Cells(i).Value
                ElseIf (i Mod 2) <> 0 Then
                    oddFS = oddFS + 2 * myRange.Cells(i).Value
        End If
        Next i

    Me.TextBox2.Text = CStr(Val(Me.TextBox1.Text) * (1 / 3) * (extremFS +
oddFS + evenFS))
    End If
```

```
End Sub
```

Nowadays there are applications, even free ones, which calculate the geometric properties of an object with high precision. These applications use photogrammetry to find the geometry of a three-dimensional body. However, the above code could be the basis for making a primitive calculator of areas or volumes knowing some ordinates.

28.24. Exercise number 24

Type: Loops for, while, do and for each.

Problem: Use the vbGreen function to shade the cells in column "A" to green, which are only equal to one, ending the process at that instant.

Solution: During the exercise, you will iterate through column A and apply green color to cells with the value changes from 1. The loop will terminate when the cell value equals 1.

6
5
10
5
10
1
10
2
6
2
1
5
44

Figure 81. Looping cell coloring example

To do this, use the following code:

```vba
Option Explicit


Sub colouring()
  Range("A1").Select
  Do While ActiveCell.Value <> 1
    ActiveCell.Offset(1, 0).Select
      If ActiveCell.Value = 1 Then
        ActiveCell.Interior.Color = vbGreen
      ElseIf ActiveCell.Value = "" Then
      Exit Do
      End If
  Loop
End Sub
```

28.25. Exercise number 25

Type: Loops for, while, do and for each.

Problem: If the value exists, find the location of a number using a UserForms of five inserted numbers.

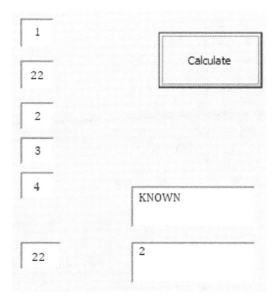

Figure 82. Location of a number inserted

Solution: To solve this exercise, create a UserForm that allows the user to insert five values. The form should then indicate whether the entered value exists and, if so, its location within the array. The following code can be used to accomplish this task:

```
Private Sub CommandButton_Click()

    Dim val(5) As Integer
    Dim z As String
    Dim a As Double

    val(1) = Me.TextBox1.Text
    val(2) = Me.TextBox2.Text
    val(3) = Me.TextBox3.Text
    val(4) = Me.TextBox4.Text
    val(5) = Me.TextBox5.Text
    val(6) = Me.TextBox6.Text

    z = "UNKNOWN"

      For i = 0 To UBound(val, 1)
        If val(i) = val(6) Then
           z = "KNOWN"
           a = i
           Exit For
        End If
      Next i

    If a <> 0 Then
       Me.TextBox8.Text = Str(i)
       ElseIf a = 0 Then
          Me.TextBox8.Text = "UNKNOWN"
    End If

    Me.TextBox7.Text = z
End Sub
```

28.26. Exercise number 26

Type: Loops for, while, do and for each.

Problem: Enter two five-letter arrays and determine how many of them match.

Solution: To solve this problem, create a UserForm where the user enters 5 + 5 letters. The program will then indicate the number of matches.

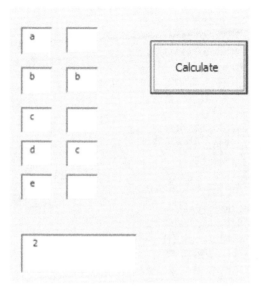

Figure 83. Example of arrays

To do this, you can use the following code:

Option Explicit

```
Private Sub CommandButton1_Click()
    Dim a As Integer
    Dim i As Integer
    Dim j As Integer
    Dim valA(4) As String
    Dim valB(4) As String

    a = 0   'Initialize the variable 'a'.

    valA(0) = Me.TextBox1.Text
    valA(1) = Me.TextBox2.Text
    valA(2) = Me.TextBox3.Text
    valA(3) = Me.TextBox4.Text
    valA(4) = Me.TextBox5.Text

    valB(0) = Me.TextBox6.Text
    valB(1) = Me.TextBox7.Text
    valB(2) = Me.TextBox8.Text
    valB(3) = Me.TextBox9.Text
    valB(4) = Me.TextBox10.Text

        For i = 0 To UBound(valA, 1)
          For j = 0 To UBound(valB, 1)
            If valA(i) <> "" & valB(j) <> "" Then
              If valA(i) = valB(j) Then
                a = a + 1
              End If
            End If
          Next j
        Next i
    Me.TextBox11.Text = Str(a)
End Sub
```

Note: The Ubound function is utilized to determine the size of an array. This function takes two arguments: the array name and the array dimension boundary → Ubound(array name, array dimension boundary). In this instance, UBound(valA, 1) equals 4. Thus, the matrix has a dimension ranging from 0 to 4. Remember that arrays start from 0.

28.27. Exercise number 27

Type: Loops for, while, do and for each.

Problem: Play a straightforward game in which the user guesses a number between 1 and 10. If the user guesses correctly, the program will congratulate them. If the user does not guess correctly, the program will indicate whether they guessed too high or too low.

Solution: This game involves creating a special UserForm named InputBox, which is an Excel function that generates a dialog box without the need for design or creation.

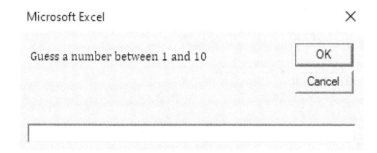

Figure 84. Guessing game

To use the program, first enter a number between 1 and 10. The InputBox contains the text: "Guess a number between 1 and 10." The program generates a random number and compares it with the number entered by the user:

```
Option Explicit
```

```
Sub guessGame()
    Dim guessNumber As Integer
    Dim userNumber As Integer
    guessNumber = Application.WorksheetFunction.RandBetween(1, 10)

    Do
    userNumber = InputBox("Guess a number between 1 and 10: ")

        If userNumber = guessNumber Then
            MsgBox "You has guessed the number! Congratulations!"
            Exit Do

        ElseIf userNumber > guessNumber Then
            MsgBox "The number is so high"
            Else
                MsgBox "The number is so low"
        End If
    Loop
End Sub
```

Note: This game is interesting because it uses the Do-Loop. The game is repeated continuously until the number is guessed, and then it ends with the 'exit do' statement.

28.28. Exercise number 28

Type: Loops for, while, do and for each.

Problem: Perform a simple exercise that stores and verifies a user-created password.

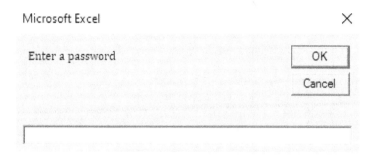

Figure 85. Creating a password

Solution: The field of passwords and cryptography can be complex, particularly for those unfamiliar with the field. This book will provide a basic introduction to these subjects without requiring a university degree or master's level knowledge. The following exercise offers a simple approach:

```
Option Explicit
```

```
Sub savePassword()

Dim savedPassword As String
Dim checkedPassword As String

savedPassword = InputBox("Insert a Password:")
MsgBox "The Password has been inserted successfully"
  Do
  checkedPassword = InputBox("Insert a Password : ")
    If savedPassword = checkedPassword Then
      MsgBox "Correct Password"
      Exit Do
    Else
      MsgBox "Incorrect Password"
      Exit Do
    End If
  Loop

End Sub
```

Note: The password is entered as a variable of type 'String' and compared with the second password entered. If they match, a dialog box will indicate this, and the 'Loop' will exit. If they do not match, the user will be prompted to re-enter the password until a match is achieved.

28.29. Exercise number 29

Type: Loops for, while, do and for each.

Problem: For each cell in column "A" create the sequential value (i.e., 1, 2, 3, 4, etc.) from the number 1 every second. To do this, create a loop that can ended by pressing the "escape" key.

Solution: The code utilizes a 'Do While' loop to fill the cells in column A with sequential numbers. A new value is added every second. The 'i' variable starts at 1 and increases by 1 for each iteration of the loop. Within the loop, the instruction 'Range("A" & i).value = i' writes the value of 'i' in the corresponding cell of the 'A' column.

```
Option Explicit
Private Declare PtrSafe Function GetAsyncKeyState Lib "user32.dll" (ByVal
vkey As Long) As Integer


Sub stopLoop()
Dim i As Integer
i = 1

    Do While True
      'Show the value of cell every second
      If Application.Wait(Now + TimeValue("0:00:01")) = True Then
        Range("A" & i).Value = i
        i = i + 1
      End If

        'Exit game when press ESC
      If GetAsyncKeyState(vbKeyEscape) <> 0 Then
        Exit Do
      End If
    Loop

End Sub
```

The reason for using 'While True' is that the loop runs continuously until it is interrupted by the execution of 'Exit Do'. This means that the loop will continue to run as long as the 'True' condition is met, which is always the case.

To exit the "Loop" the user must press the "ESC" key. The code employs the "GetAsyKeyState" function to check if the Escape key is pressed, the "Loop" is interrupted by the "Exit Do" entry.

The VBA function 'Private Declare PtrSafe Function GetAsyncKeyState Lib 'user32.dll' (ByVal vKey As Long) As Integer' allows the user to access the Windows operating system function 'GetAsyncKeyState', which returns information about the state of a key on the keyboard. The function takes an integer argument 'vKey', which specifies the code of the key to be checked and returns an integer value indicating whether the key has been pressed. The 'Declare' keyword is used to indicate that an external function is being used in the VBA code. The 'PtrSafe' keyword is used to ensure compatibility with both 32-bit and 64-bit versions of Microsoft Office. The 'user32.dll' part of the Lib indicates the name of the dynamic binding library that contains the GetAsyncKeyState function. This library is a file that contains the list of functions and resources used by various programs.

Finally, the code waits for one second before displaying the number sequence. To adjust the timeout, simply modify the value of '0:00:01' to your desired duration.

28.30. Exercise number 30

Type: Loops for, while, do and for each.

Problem: Generate the Fibonacci series of "N" elements, knowing that the *Fibonacci* series satisfies that each current element of the series is the result of the sum of the previous two: $a_n = a_{n-1} + a_{n-2}$. Then, calculate the error for each a_n knowing that the ratio $a_n/a_{n-1} \approx (1 + \sqrt{5})/2$.

Solution: The Fibonacci series is an infinite mathematical sequence discovered by Italian mathematician Leonardo Fibonacci in the 13th century while studying rabbit breeding. This series has many interesting properties as it is found in nature, such as in the arrangement of tree branches, the spiral of snail shells, the seeds of a sunflower, and the human body. It is also present in architecture, including the Sagrada Familia in Barcelona. The Fibonacci series has applications in cryptography, finance, and fractal mathematics. The Fibonacci series is closely related to the golden ratio, which is approximately equal to $(1 + \sqrt{5})/2 \approx 1.618033989....$

The subject has a broad biography that extends to various fields, including engineering, physics, architecture, medicine, and philosophy. However, this is a modest example that may be useful to VBA students.

The series starts with the first two numbers being 1 and 2, so the expression $a_n = a_{n-1} + a_{n-2}$ applies when $n \geq 2$

Calculation	Serial Value	Golden Ratio	Error
1	1	-	-
2	2	2	-23,6067977500 %
3 = 2 + 1	3	1,5	7,2949016875 %
5 = 3 + 2	5	1,66666667	-3,0056647916 %
8 = 5 + 3	8	1,6	1,1145618000 %
13 = 8 + 5	13	1,625	-0,4305231719 %
21 = 13 + 8	21	1,61538462	0,1637402789 %
34 = 21 + 13	34	1,61904762	-0,0626457976 %
55 = 34 + 21	55	1,61764706	0,0239135846 %
89 = 55 + 34	89	1,61818182	-0,0091363613 %
144 = 89 + 55	144	1,61797753	0,0034894607 %
233 = 144 + 89	233	1,61805556	-0,0013329019 %
377 = 233 + 144	377	1,61802575	0,0005091164 %

Table 14. Fibonacci series

As you can see, the error decreases as more values are obtained from the series. For a value of 102334155, the error is 0.00000000000000137231%.

Create an InputBox to enter the number of items in the series. Then, column A will display a sequence number, column B will show the series values, column C will indicate the relationship a_n/a_n-1, and column D will display any errors.

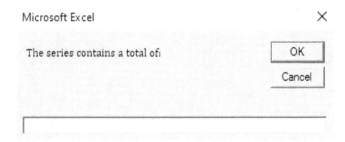

Figure 86. Generating a Fibonacci series of "N" elements

A code would be:

Option Explicit

```vb
Sub Fibonacci()

Dim item As Integer
Dim i As Integer
Dim goldenNumber As Double

goldenNumber = (1 + (5 ^ 0.5)) / 2 'Calculate the exact value of the golden ratio
item = InputBox("The number of elements contained in the series is: ") 'we enter the number of items

    Do While i < item
    i = i + 1 'For each iteration the unit is added
    Cells(i, 1).Value = i

        If i <= 2 Then ' We enter the values for the first two items of the series
        Cells(1, 2).Value = 1
        Cells(1, 3).Value = 0
        Cells(2, 2).Value = 2
        Cells(2, 3).Value = 2
        Cells(2, 4).Value = 100 * (goldenNumber - Cells(i, 3).Value) /
goldenNumber

        ElseIf i > 2 Then ' we calculate the rest of the items in the series greater
than the first two values of the series

        Cells(i, 2).Value = Cells(i - 1, 2).Value + Cells(i - 2, 2).Value 'Fibonacci
value
        Cells(i, 3).Value = Cells(i, 2).Value 'Fibonacci value
        Cells(i, 4).Value = 100 * (goldenNumber - Cells(i, 3).Value) /
goldenNumber 'Calculated error

        End If

    Loop
End Sub
```

28.31. Exercise number 31

Type: Functions, procedures, and sub-algorithms

Problem: Make the product of any two numbers using a function.

Solution: To perform the function, use parameters per value to ensure that the main program is not interconnected with the function. If parameter values are changed within the function, they will not be changed in the main program.

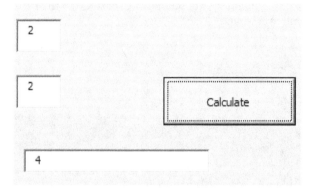

Figure 87. Product of two numbers

The code could look like this:

```
Private Sub calculate_Click()

    Dim a As Double
    Dim b As Double
    Dim c As Double

    a = Va1(Me.TextBox1.Text)
    b = Va1(Me.TextBox2.Text)
    c = product(a, b)
    Me.textBox3.Text = c

End Sub
```

```
Private Function product(ByVal input1 As Double, ByVal input2 As Double)
As Double

    Dim c As Double
    c = input1 * input2
    product = c

End Function
```

28.32. Exercise number 32

Type: Functions, procedures, and sub-algorithms

Problem: Calculate the product of four numbers by using a function and a one-dimensional vector.

Solution: To complete this exercise, create a UserForm where you can input four values and multiply them together. It is important to note that the function must have an array as a byRef argument.

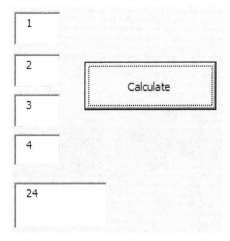

Figure 88. Product of four numbers

The code could be this:

```vb
Private Sub calculate_Click()
    Dim p(3) As Double
    Dim r As Double

    p(0) = Val(Me.TextBox1.Text)
    p(1) = Val(Me.TextBox2.Text)
    p(2) = Val(Me.TextBox3.Text)
    p(3) = Val(Me.TextBox4.Text)

    r = product(p)
    Me.TextBox5.Text = r

End Sub
```

```vb
Private Function product(ByRef myInput() As Double) As Double
    Dim c As Double
    Dim i As Integer
    c = 1 'If "c" was null, the result always will be 0.
        For i = 0 To UBound(myInput, 1)
            c = c * myInput(i)
            product = c
        Next i
End Function
```

28.33. Exercise number 33

Type: Functions, procedures, and sub-algorithms

Problem: Given two matrices A and B of 3 x 3, obtain the product of those matrices. Solve the problem by using a function.

Solution: To solve the exercise, create a UserForm where you enter the values of the arrays and display the result:

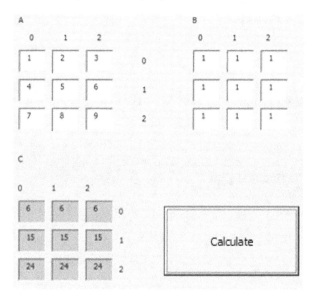

Figure 89. Product of two matrices

You can use the following code:

Option Explicit

Private Sub CommandButton1_Click()

```
    Dim a(2, 2) As Integer
    Dim b(2, 2) As Integer
    Dim c() As Integer

    'Get the data. Note: The ":" can be used to reduce the number of lines.
    a(0, 0) = Val(Me.textBox1.Text): a(0, 1) = Val(Me.TextBox2.Text)
    a(0, 2) = Val(Me.textBox3.Text): a(1, 0) = Val(Me.TextBox4.Text)
    a(1, 1) = Val(Me.textBox5.Text): a(1, 2) = Val(Me.TextBox6.Text)
    a(2, 0) = Val(Me.tcxtBox7.Text): a(2, 1) = Val(Me.TextBox8.Text)
    a(2, 2) = Val(Me.textBox9.Text)


    b(0, 0) = Val(Me.textBox10.Text): b(0, 1) = Val(Me.TextBox11.Text)
    b(0, 2) = Val(Me.textBox12.Text): b(1, 0) = Val(Me.TextBox13.Text)
    b(1, 1) = Val(Me.textBox14.Text): b(1, 2) = Val(Me.TextBox15.Text)
    b(2, 0) = Val(Me.textBox16.Text): b(2, 1) = Val(Me.TextBox17.Text)
    b(2, 2) = Val(Me.textBox18.Text)

    c = matrixProduct(a, b)

    Me.textBox19.Text = c(0, 0): Me.TextBox20.Text = c(0, 1)
    Me.textBox21.Text = c(0, 2): Me.TextBox22.Text = c(1, 0)
    Me.textBox23.Text = c(1, 1): Me.TextBox24.Text = c(1, 2)
    Me.textBox25.Text = c(2, 0): Me.TextBox26.Text = c(2, 1)
    Me.textBox27.Text = c(2, 2)

End Sub
```

```
Private Function matrixProduct(ByRef MatrixA() As Integer, ByRef MatrixB()
As Integer) As Integer()

    Dim i As Integer
    Dim j As Integer
    Dim k As Integer
    Dim d(2, 2) As Integer

    'Matrix product
    For i = 0 To 2
        For j = 0 To 2
```

```
    For k = 0 To 2
        d(i, j) = d(i, j) + MatrixA(i, k) * MatrixB(k, j)
      Next k
   Next j
 Next i

 matrixProduct = d

End Function
```

This problem is intriguing because it enables the solution of matrix products, which is particularly useful in engineering and mathematics. For instance, in structural calculations, solving structures using the matrix method is of great interest.

28.34. Exercise number 34

Type: Functions, procedures, and sub-algorithms

Problem: Obtain the subtraction of matrices A and B, both of size 3 x 3, a function must be used.

Solution: To complete this task, create a 'UserForm' that allows users to input matrix values and view the resulting output.

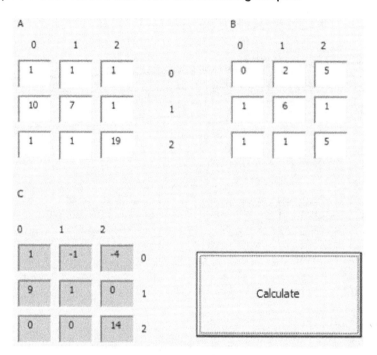

Figure 90. Subtraction of two matrix

The following code can be used:

```
Option Explicit

-
Private Sub CommandButton1_Click()

    Dim a(2, 2) As Integer
    Dim b(2, 2) As Integer
    Dim c() As Integer
```

```
'getting the data. Note: The ":" allow to reduce the number of lines
a(0, 0) = Val(Me.textBox1.Text): a(0, 1) = Val(Me.TextBox2.Text)
a(0, 2) = Val(Me.textBox3.Text): a(1, 0) = Val(Me.TextBox4.Text)
a(1, 1) = Val(Me.textBox5.Text): a(1, 2) = Val(Me.TextBox6.Text)
a(2, 0) = Val(Me.textBox7.Text): a(2, 1) = Val(Me.TextBox8.Text)
a(2, 2) = Val(Me.textBox9.Text)

b(0, 0) = Val(Me.textBox10.Text): b(0, 1) = Val(Me.TextBox11.Text)
b(0, 2) = Val(Me.textBox12.Text): b(1, 0) = Val(Me.TextBox13.Text)
b(1, 1) = Val(Me.textBox14.Text): b(1, 2) = Val(Me.TextBox15.Text)
b(2, 0) = Val(Me.textBox16.Text): b(2, 1) = Val(Me.TextBox17.Text)
b(2, 2) = Val(Me.textBox18.Text)

c = matrixSubtraction(a, b)

Me.textBox19.Text = c(0, 0): Me.TextBox20.Text = c(0, 1)
Me.textBox21.Text = c(0, 2): Me.TextBox22.Text = c(1, 0)
Me.textBox23.Text = c(1, 1): Me.TextBox24.Text = c(1, 2)
Me.textBox25.Text = c(2, 0): Me.TextBox26.Text = c(2, 1)
Me.textBox27.Text = c(2, 2)

End Sub
```

```
Private Function matrixSubtraction(ByRef MatrixA() As Integer, ByRef
MatrixB() As Integer) As Integer()

Dim i As Integer
Dim j As Integer
Dim d(2, 2) As Integer

'Matrix product
For i = 0 To 2
  For j = 0 To 2
      d(i, j) = MatrixA(i, j) - MatrixB(i, j)
  Next j
Next i

matrixProduct = d

End Function
```

Note: As with the previous exercise, matrix addition and subtraction are essential in the scientific and technical fields.

28.35. Exercise number 35

Type: Functions, procedures, and sub-algorithms

Problem: Enter four values in a 2 x 2 array and get the lowest number entered. Use a function to solve the problem.

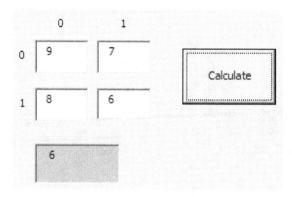

Figure 91. Minor of a four-element array

Solution: To solve the problem, create a 'UserForms' like the illustrated above. Insert four values and the smallest value will be displayed as the result. The code is as follows:

```vb
Option Explicit
```

```vb
Private Sub Calcule_Click()
    Dim s As Integer

    'Declare the matrix dimensions as 2 x 2.
    Dim m(1, 1) As Integer

    'Inputs
    m(0, 0) = Val(Me.textbox1.Text)
    m(0, 1) = Val(Me.textbox2.Text)
    m(1, 0) = Val(Me.textbox3.Text)
    m(1, 1) = Val(Me.textbox4.Text)

    'Calling the function
    s = minor(m)

    'Display the result
    Me.textbox5.Text = Str(s)

End Sub
```

```vb
Private Function minor(ByRef myMatrix() As Integer) As Integer
    Dim s As Integer
    Dim i As Integer
    Dim j As Integer

    s = myMatrix(0, 0) 's Compare's every value.
    For i = 0 To 1
        For j = 0 To 1
            If myMatrix(i, j) < s Then
                s = myMatrix(i, j)
            End If
        Next j
    Next i

End Function
```

28.36. Exercise number 36

Type: Functions, procedures, and sub-algorithms

Problem: Create a subroutine named 'example' with two arguments: variable 1 and variable 2. Variable 1 should be passed by reference, while variable 2 should be passed by value. A dialog box should display how the variables' values are changed or kept in the main program.

Solution: To complete this exercise, you need to create two blocks: a main program and an 'example' function or subroutine. The 'example' subroutine should have two arguments: 'variable1' and 'variable2'. 'Variable1' is passed by reference, which means that any changes made inside the subroutine will be presented in the original variable outside the subroutine. Variable2, on the other hand, is passed by value. This means that any changes made to Variable2 inside the subroutine will not affect the original variable outside the subroutine. In the main procedure, two variables, 'a' and 'b', are declared and assigned a value of 1. The subroutine 'example' is then called, passing 'a' and 'b' as arguments. Within the subroutine, the values of 'variable1' and 'variable2' are incremented in the unit. After executing the subroutine, the program prints the values of 'a' and 'b'. In this scenario, 'a' is incremented by one since it is passed by reference, while 'b' remains unchanged because it is passed by value.

```
Sub main()

    Dim a As Integer
    Dim b As Integer

    a = 1
    b = 1

    example a, b
    MsgBox "variable 1 out from subroutine.: "
    MsgBox "variable 2 out from subroutine.: "

End Sub
```

```
Sub example(ByRef variable1 As Integer, ByVal variable2 As Integer)

    Variable1 = variable1+ 1
    variable2 = variable2 + 1
    MsgBox "variable 1 inside of subroutine.: " & variable1
    MsgBox "variable 2 inside of subroutine.: " & variable2

End Sub
```

28.37. Exercise number 37

Type: Functions, procedures, and sub-algorithms

Problem: Create a function to concatenate three consecutive cells and separate the content using a hyphen. If the last cell is empty, only concatenate the first two adjacent cells.

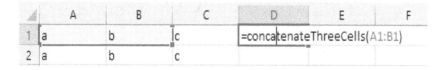

	A	B	C	D	E	F
1	a	b	c	=concatenateThreeCells(A1:B1)		
2	a	b	c			

Figure 92. Example of a three-element concatenation

Solution: Excel has a wide range of functions, including Vlookup, SUMIF, and COUNTA. However, if you need to create a custom function, you can do so by going to Insert -> Module and entering the appropriate code.

```
Option Explicit


Function concatenateThreeCells(myRange As Range) As String

  If myRange.Cells(1, 3) <> "" Then

    concatenateThreeCells = myRange.Cells(1, 1) & "-" & myRange.Cells(1, 2)
& "-" & myRange.Cells(1, 3)

    ElseIf myRange.Cells(1, 3) = " " Then

      concatenateThreeCells = myRange.Cells(1, 1) & "-" & myRange.Cells(1,
2)

  End If

End Function
```

Note: Excel formulas should be created in modules rather than in sheets in the VBA editor. This is because custom formulas are intended to be used in multiple spreadsheets. Placing them in one module makes them available to all worksheets in a workbook.

28.38. Exercise number 38

Type: Graphics

Problem: Represent a five-pointed star using Excel's "Shape" function.

Solution: The code below will create a yellow five-pointed star at X = 100, Y = 100. The star will have a width and height of 100 units, a red border with a line width of three units, and a round dotted line style.

Figure 93. Depiction of a five-pointed star with ornate details

```
Option Explicit


Sub drawStar()

Dim mySheet As Worksheet
Set mySheet = ActiveSheet

Dim myShape As Shape
Set myShape = mySheet.Shapes.AddShape(msoShape5pointStar, 100, 100,
100, 100)

   With myShape

      .Fill.Visible = msoTrue
      .Fill.ForeColor.RGB = RGB(255, 255, 0)  'Yellow Color
      .Line.Weight = 3
      .Line.DashStyle = msoLineRoundDot
      .Line.ForeColor.RGB = RGB(255, 0, 0) 'red color

   End With

End Sub
```

Note: This exercise is interesting because it teaches how to represent shapes in Excel, generate colors using RGB, and use 'with' to give the star custom characteristics. Shapes can be interesting for many reasons, for example, it allows you to highlight a line in your table, create custom charts, create flowcharts, presentations, or aids in any situation in which you need to represent data or ideas in a visual or attractive way.

28.39. Exercise number 39

Type: Graphics

Problem: Plot a histogram using data from a spreadsheet and format the title alongside the axis titles.

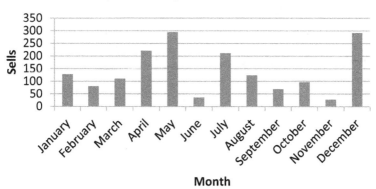

Figure 94. Generating graphics with VBA

Solution: To plot a histogram in VBA, use the 'shapes' class method to add a new chart object to the spreadsheet. This method is an updated version of the previous 'AddChart' method. When using 'AddChart2', specify 'xlColumnClustered' as an argument to create a chart of grouped columns. The number '240' refers to the specific type of chart of grouped columns. Experiment with different numbers to explore the available options.

```
Option Explicit


Sub newChart()

' Select data
Sheets("Sheet1").Range("A1:B12").Select

' Insert Chart
ActiveSheet.Shapes.AddChart(240, xlColumnC1ustered).Select
```

```vba
' Formatting Chart
   With ActiveChart
     .HasTitle = True
     .ChartTitle.Text = "Monthly Incomes"
     .Axes(xlCategory).HasTitle = True
     .Axes(xlCategory).AxisTitle.Text = "Month"
     .Axes(xlValue).HasTitle = True
     .Axes(xlValue).AxisTitle.Text = "Sells"
   End With

End Sub
```

28.40. Exercise number 40

Type: Graphics

Problem: Create a progress bar that displays the status of a program as it runs. The program should be initiated by clicking a button.

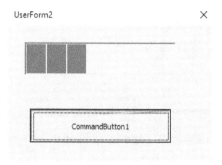

Figure 95. Generating a progress Bar

Solution: To solve this problem, first create a userForm with a button that, when pressed, runs a program. Then add the progress bar as follows:

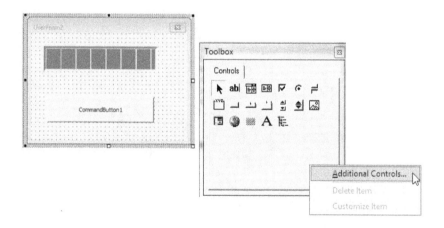

Figure 96. Generating a progress bar with a UserForm

While running the program, the Microsoft ProgressBar Control may not be visible. If this is the case, right-click on 'Additional Controls' and select the synonymous control from the list.

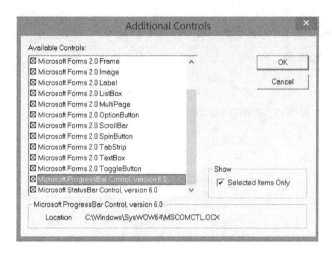

Figure 97. Adding additional controls

The code below calculates a percentage as an "integer" and performs 10,000 iterations to slow down the progression of the bar. Finally, the percentage value is rounded to remove decimals using the 'round' function.

```
Option Explicit
```

```
Private Sub ComandButton1_Click ( )

' Define variables
Dim i As Long
Dim n As Long
Dim percentage As Integer

' Define the number of iterations

        n = 10000

        ' Perform the loop

        For i = 0 To n

                ' Calculate percentage of progress
                percentage = Round (i / n * 100, 0)

                ' Update progress bar
                Controls ("ProgressBar1") . Value = percentage

                DoEvents

        Next i
End Sub
```

28.41. Exercise number 41

Type: Graphics

Problem: Create a game of telepong, also known as ping-pong. To accomplish this, establish a playing area and a ball that remains within the boundaries and bounces when it encounters with a paddle.

Solution: In this exercise we will embark on a fascinating journey to the origins of the world of video games with the classic Pong or Telepong. From the humble beginnings of "Tennis for Two" in 1958 to the commercial explosion of Pong in 1972. We will discover how this simple game launched a digital revolution.

This exercise explores the evolution of Telepong and provides a step-by-step guide to creating your own Ping-Pong game in Microsoft Excel. The guide covers ball movement and paddle control in detail.

Pong or Telepong: A journey to the origins of video games

In the digital age, with high-definition graphics and immersive gaming experiences, it is interesting to explore the humble beginnings of video games. Pong, or telepong, was one of the pioneers that marked the beginning of this revolution.

The Origin: Pong

Pong, also known as Tele-Pong, is a video game that belongs to the first generation of video consoles and games. In 1958, American physicist William Higinbotham created a pioneering game called 'Tennis for Two' on an oscilloscope, which laid the groundwork for virtual video games. A decade later, Nolan Bushnell, who worked at the famous Atari company, made Pong a commercial reality and launched it on the market on November 29, 1972.

Figure 98. William Higinbotham

Figure 99. Nolan Bushnell

Pong is a video game based on the sport of ping-pong. The game involves two players using rackets to bounce a ball on a table. Despite its simplicity, Pong's commercial success laid the foundations of the million-dollar video game industry. The first versions of Pong were based on oscilloscopes and basic electronics, from a 21st-century perspective.

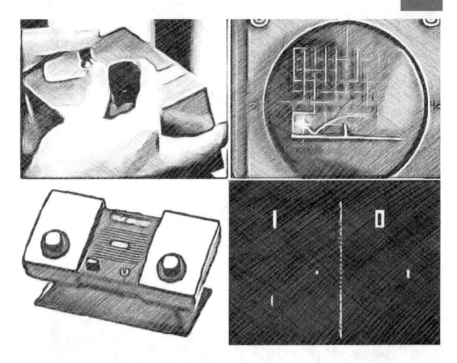

Figure 100. Evolution of the game of pong

Evolution: Telepong

Over time, technology has advanced and given way to new gaming experiences. Telepong emerged as an improved version of Pong, incorporating innovative features. Now, players can not only control the paddles but also participate in exciting online competitions. Telepong has brought a social dimension to the world of video games, paving the way for future innovations in the industry.

Pong for scientific purposes

Elon Musk's company Neuralink has used this game for scientific purposes to evaluate the transmission of data between a primate's brain and a computer through brain implants, without the need for limb movement.

The method used is intriguing. At first, primates with brain implants are taught to play using joysticks. Once the animal has learned how to play, they are deceived. The usual command is given, but the positions of the racket are controlled by the brain. The joystick is then disconnected, even if the animal is still holding it.

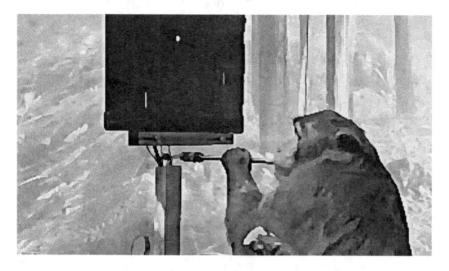

Figure 101. Experiments with primates & pong

Some papers have reported that some primates died due to complications with the implants. These complications included infections, paralysis, loss of coordination and balance, and depression.

The company Neuralink aims to develop a device that can treat patients with neurological disabilities. This device consists of wires and electrodes that enable brain-computer communication, which would benefit disabled individuals with mobility issues or conditions like epilepsy. Additionally, this interface could provide access to brain information and enhance memory. In summary, the device resembles something from a science-fiction novel.

Now, you can! The Pong Game for Excel in Visual Basic for Applications (VBA)

The game can be approached in several ways, with multiple solutions, and can be made as complicated as desired. The solution is not unique; for instance, the number of players, balls, ways of scoring, and colors can vary.

To simplify the problem and the game, we will reduce the complexity. Instead of having two players and two rackets, the user will only play against the computer with a single racket. The user can then extend and complicate the code as desired.

To accomplish this, the boundaries of the playing area where the ball will bounce are first defined. Then, the ball is created by moving every half second. To exit the game, press the 'ESC' escape key.

The *"shapes"* method is used to create the field, ball, and paddle. Pressing the up and down keys on the keyboard will cause the racket to ascend and descend with a specified speed.

The ball moves in both vertical and horizontal directions simultaneously, resulting in diagonal movement, like rebounds. When the ball touches the racket or reaches the edge of the field, the direction of movement is reversed.

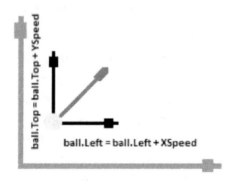

Figure 102. Composition of movement

The representation of the playing area, the ball and the shovel are also quite simple. Vertical and horizontal bars made with the "shapes" method of Excel allow you to create the playing area and the racket. The ball is also performed with the same method. The following image shows how the game is displayed:

The playing area, ball, and racket are represented in a simple manner. Refer to the image below for a visual representation: The playing area and racket are created using vertical and horizontal bars made with the 'shapes' method of Excel. The ball is also created using the same method.

Figure 103. Playground

Before beginning to program the code, it is important to write the following statement, which it will be the first instruction:

```
Option Explicit
```

To prevent the omission of any variables that engage in the game, it is important to declare all of them. Although the above instruction may not be present, any omission of constants and variables could result in errors.

Next, the focus is on game control. To achieve this, a key press must trigger an action. For instance, pressing the *'escape'* key should stop the game, while using the up and down arrow keys allows for racket control.

```
Private Declare PtrSafe Function GetAsyncKeyState Lib "user32.dll" (ByVal
vKey As Long) As Integer
```

The above statement declares the *GetAsyncKeyState* function of the user32.dll library. This function allows retrieving the status of a specific key. The term *'PtrSafe'* indicates that the statement is safe for 64-bit platforms. The function returns an integer indicating whether the key has been pressed or not. The available keys include alphanumeric, function, arrow, control, and modification keys, among others.

After completing the steps, the next task is to define all variables. This includes determining the characteristics, properties, and functions of each element. For instance, the playing area, consisting of the leftColumn, rightColumn, bottomColumn, topColumn, racket, and ball, is defined as shapes. Additionally, the boundaries of the field, such as the topLimit, bottomLimit, rightLimit, and leftLimit, are established. The ball must be visible to the eyes and therefore needs to be thrown at a specific speed. This is achieved by adjusting the variables XSpeed, YSpeed, and velPaddle. Velocity is dependent on time, which is controlled by the variables PauseTime, Start, Finish, and TotalTime.

After declaring the necessary variables and game controls, the next step is to consider the game's start. Typically, the playing area is cleared of any remnants from previous games. To achieve this, we use the following loop to remove all shapes.

```
For Each shp In ActiveSheet.Shapes
 shp.Delete
Next shp
```

Later, the playing area will be reconstructed by redrawing all the field boundaries. To accomplish this, use the following statement to create a rectangular object in the active worksheet (ActiveSheet):

```
Set leftColumn = ActiveSheet.Shapes.AddShape(msoShapeRectangle, 0, 0, 10, 210)
```

- Shapes.AddShapes: This method adds a rectangular shape to the spreadsheet.
- msoShapeRectangle: This autoshape represents a rectangle with coordinates 0, 0, 10, 20. The rectangle is created in the upper left corner of the spreadsheet with a width of 10 units and a height of 210 units.

The entire court and racket are created using the same methodology. To draw the ball, a special type of autoshape called *msoShapeOval* is used.

So far, the shapes, playing area, ball, and racket have been defined. Now, the game needs to be brought to life by making the ball move, bounce, and the racket move vertically. The game is played in two dimensions within a 'Do While True' loop that can only be scaped by pressing the *'Escape'* key. To achieve this, we will define simultaneous vertical and horizontal movements, marked by a timer that allows the ball to be observed.

In VBA, the 'Do While True' statement is used to create an infinite loop that runs continuously until a desired output condition is reached. To prevent the code from running indefinitely without the possibility of exiting quickly, easily, and securely, it is imperative to have a way to exit. This can be achieved through a conditional that executes the 'Exit Do' statement. In this case, the game can only be left by pressing the ESC key.

- **Move the ball horizontally and control the bounce of the racket:** To move the position of the ball to the left, add the horizontal velocity (Xspeed). If the ball's position exceeds the left limit ("leftLimit") or falls below the right limit ("rightLimit"), reverse the direction by multiplying the speed by -1.

```
ball.Left = ball.Left + XSpeed
  If ball.Left < leftLimit Then
    XSpeed = XSpeed * -1
  ElseIf(ball.Left + ball.Width - 5) > rightLimit or ball.Left > 175 _
            And (ball.Top - 5) >= Paddle .Top And ball.Top <= (Paddle .Top +
50) Then
                XSpeed = XSpeed * -1
  End If
```

- **Move the ball vertically and control the vertical bounce:** To adjust the ball's top position, add the vertical velocity ('YSpeed'). If the top position exceeds the vertical limits ('topLimit' or 'bottomLimit'), the vertical position will be reversed.

```
ball.Top = ball.Top + YSpeed

If ball.Top < topLimit Then
  YSpeed = YSpeed * -1
ElseIf (ball.Top + ball.Height - 5) > bottomLimit Then
  YSpeed = YSpeed * -1
End If
```

- **Stop the ball for a period to make its speed observable to the human eye:** A pause time, referred to as 'pauseTime', is defined in seconds. The 'timer' function is then used to set the 'Start' time. A 'Do While' loop is employed, along with the 'Do events' function, to wait until the current timer is greater than the initial time plus the pause duration ('PauseTime'). Upon exiting the pause loop, the 'Finish' time is recorded using the 'Timer' function.

```
PauseTime = 0.1  'Set duration in seconds
Start = Timer    'Set initial time
Do While Timer < Start + PauseTime
   DoEvents 'Go to other processes
Loop
```

```
Finish = Timer 'End time
```

Stoppage time is crucial as it prevents the ball from moving extremely fast. The computer reads instructions from top to bottom at on established speed which depend on its processor.

28.41.1. Scoring

The importance of scoring cannot be overstated. While the book presents this game in a simple and intuitive way, it can become as complicated as desired. Practicing punctuation is a valuable exercise for those looking to learn how to code or it improve their writing.

Scoring in this game is achieved by awarding a point each time the ball bounces off the racket. To determine this, a condition is required to verify the positions of the ball, specifically its left and top positions relative to the size and position of the racket. The resulting score is displayed in cell 'E1' on the game sheet.

```
If ball.Left > 175 And (ball.Top - 5) >= Paddle .Top And ball.Top <= (Paddle
.Top + 50) Then
'We define the scoring system
   Dim i As Integer
   i = i + 1
   Range("E1").Value = i
End If
```

The code checks whether the ball's position is beyond a certain horizontal limit and if the vertical position of the ball is within the upper and lower limits of the racket. If this condition is met, the variable 'i' is incremented, and the value in cell 'E1' is updated.

In the following section of the code, the *GetAsyncKeyState* function is used to detect the pressing of the *'up'* arrow (vbKeyUp). If this is the case and the top racket position (Paddle.top) is greater than ten, the top racket position is decreased according to the racket speed.

```
If GetAsyncKeyState(vbKeyUp) Then 'With this line, we control the raising
and lowering of the shovel
  If Paddle .Top > 10 Then 'With this instruction the racket does not leave the
playing area
    direcPaddle = -1
    Paddle .Top = Paddle .Top - velPaddle
  End If
End If
```

Finally, the game can be ended by pressing the escape key.

```
If GetAsyncKeyState(vbKeyEscape) <> 0 Then
  Exit Do
End If
```

With all characteristics in mind, we can now include the complete code:

```
Option Explicit
Private Declare PtrSafe Function GetAsyncKeyState Lib "user32.dll" (ByVal
vKey As Long) As Integer

Sub pong()

'We define the shapes as the margins of the field, ball, and paddles.
  Dim ball As Shape
  Dim leftColumn As Shape
  Dim rightColumn As Shape
  Dim bottomColumn As Shape
  Dim topColumn As Shape
  Dim paddle As Shape

'This variable allows you to eliminate all previous forms.
  Dim shp As Shape

'We define the boundaries of the field.
```

```vb
Dim topLimit As Integer
Dim bottomLimit As Integer
Dim rightLimit As Integer
Dim leftLimit As Integer

'Select ball speed.
Dim XSpeed As Integer
Dim YSpeed As Integer
Dim velPaddle As Integer

'Define the refresh time rate to be visible to eyes.
Dim PauseTime, Start, Finish, TotalTime As Long

'This variable allows to control the movement up & down of Paddle.
Dim direcPaddle As Integer

'Define the shape and speed of Paddle.
velPaddle = 10

'Define field limits
topLimit = 15
bottomLimit = 190
leftLimit = 15
rightLimit = 200

'Define speed ball
XSpeed = 5
YSpeed = 5

    'When starting the program eliminate all shapes.
    For Each shp In ActiveSheet.Shapes
        shp.Delete
    Next shp

' First, draw the playing area and add the columns with the "shapes"
method.
    ' Consider that: Position X, Position Y, Width, height
    Set leftColumn = ActiveSheet.Shapes.AddShape(msoShapeRectangle, 0, 0,
10, 210)
    leftColumn.Fill.ForeColor.RGB = RGB(192, 192, 192)

    Set rightColumn = ActiveSheet.Shapes.AddShape(msoShapeRectangle, 210,
0, 10, 210)
    rightColumn.Fill.ForeColor.RGB = RGB(192, 192, 192)

    Set topColumn = ActiveSheet.Shapes.AddShape(msoShapeRectangle, 10, 0,
200, 10)
```

```vba
    rightColumn.Fill.ForeColor.RGB = RGB(192, 192, 192)

    Set bottomColumn = ActiveSheet.Shapes.AddShape(msoShapeRectangle,
10, 200, 200, 10)
    rightColumn.Fill.ForeColor.RGB = RGB(192, 192, 192)

    'Draw the Paddle
    Set Paddle  = ActiveSheet.Shapes.AddShape(msoShapeRectangle, 200, 100,
10, 50)
    rightColumn.Fill.ForeColor.RGB = RGB(192, 192, 192)

    ' Draw the ball: Initial position X, initial position Y, Length, Width
    Set ball = ActiveSheet.Shapes.AddShape(msoShapeOval, 10, 50, 20, 20)
    ball.Fill.ForeColor.RGB = RGB(255, 255, 0)

    ' Give movement to the ball
    Do While True

        'Move the ball horizontally and control horizontal bounce
        ball.Left = ball.Left + XSpeed

        If ball.Left < leftLimit Then
            XSpeed = XSpeed * -1
            ElseIf (ball.Left + ball.Width - 5) > rightLimit Or ball.Left > 175 _
            And (ball.Top - 5) >= Paddle .Top And ball.Top <= (Paddle .Top +
50) Then
                XSpeed = XSpeed * -1
        End If

        'Move the ball vertically and control vertical bounce.
        ball.Top = ball.Top + YSpeed

        If ball.Top < topLimit Then
            YSpeed = YSpeed * -1
            ElseIf (ball.Top + ball.Height - 5) > bottomLimit Then
                YSpeed = YSpeed * -1
        End If

'Stop for a certain time so that the ball goes at a speed observable to the eyes.
        PauseTime = 0.1 'Set duration in terms of second
        Start = Timer    'Set initial time
        Do While Timer < Start + PauseTime
            DoEvents 'Go to other processes
        Loop
        Finish = Timer  'End Time

    'Scooring
```

```
    If ball.Left > 175 And (ball.Top - 5) >= Paddle .Top And ball.Top <=
(Paddle .Top + 50) Then
        'Define the scoring system
        Dim i As Integer
        i = i + 1
        Range("E1").Value = i

    End If

    If GetAsyncKeyState(vbKeyUp) Then 'With this instruction, we control the
raising and lowering of the blade
        If Paddle .Top > 10 Then 'With this line the Paddle does not leave the
playing area
            direcPaddle = -1
            Paddle .Top = Paddle .Top - velPaddle

        End If
    End If

    If GetAsyncKeyState(vbKeyDown) Then
        If Paddle .Top < 150 Then 'With this line the Paddle does not leave the
playing area             direcPaddle = 1
            Paddle .Top = Paddle .Top + velPaddle
        End If
    End If

    'By pressing Scape, we exit the game.
    If GetAsyncKeyState(vbKeyEscape) <> 0 Then
        Exit Do
    End If

    Loop
End Sub
```

28.41.2. Legacy and reflections

Pong and Telepong are timeless reminders of how simplicity can be the key to success. These simple yet ingenious games paved the way for the video game industry we know today. Evolving from oscilloscope screens to online multiplayer experiences, they have left a legacy. Not only have these games entertained millions of young people and adults, but they also laid the foundation for today's rich and diverse video game industry.

28.42. Exercise number 42

Type: Multimedia

Problem: Make a program that runs a media file in Excel VBA.

Solution: There are various methods to approach this exercise, but an error-free approach is to use a Unique Object Identifier (UUID), also known as a Global Unique Identifier (GUID). This GUID is associated with Microsoft's Windows Media Player and uses the 'IWMPPlayer4' interface provided by the 'WMPlayer.OCX.7' object library, identified by the GUID 6BF52A52-394A-11d3-B153-00C04F79FAA6.

```
Option Explicit


Sub musicPlayer()

        Dim WMP As Object
        Set WMP = CreateObject("new: {6BF52A52-394A-11d3-B153-
00C04F79FAA6}")
        WMP.openPlayer =
"C:\Users\XXXXXX\XXXX\YYYYY\ZZZZZ\HH.mp4"

End Sub
```

Note: The provided code allows for a wide range of possibilities and wings the imagination. For instance, it can be adapted to play songs listed in an Excel column by inputting their respective URLs.

28.43. Exercise number 43

Type: Multimedia

Problem: Running a program that runs a Windows error sound.

Solution: To write code that plays a Windows error sound when running a program, use the "sndPlaySound" function of the Windows API:

```
Option Explicit

#If VBA7 Then
Private Declare PtrSafe Function sndPlaySound Lib "winmm.dll" Alias
"sndPlaySoundA" (ByVal lpszSoundName As String, ByVal uFlags As Long) As
Long
#Else
Private Declare Function sndPlaySound Lib "winmm.dll" Alias
"sndPlaySoundA" (ByVal lpszSoundName As String, ByVal uFlags As Long) As
Long
#End If


Sub soundPlayer()
    Call sndPlaySound("C:\Windows\Media\Windows Hardware Fail.wav", 1)
End Sub
```

However, it is important to note that the above VBA code may fail to run if the path does not exist in the Windows\Media location or if the 'winmm.dll' library is unavailable. To allow for alternative sound selection, the reader can choose a different path. The code may vary slightly depending on the operating system's version (32-bit or 64-bit), which is why an 'if' statement is used to identify the system version.

The 'sndPlaySound' function is a Windows API function that can be used in Excel's VBA to play sounds. The function's basic syntax requires the path of the sound file and a flag, which can be one of the following: SND_ASYNC, SND_LOOP, SND_MEMORY, SND_NODEFAULT (value 0), SND_NOSTOP, SND_SENTRY, SND_SYNC, or SND_SYSTEM. For more information and a detailed explanation of each flag's possibilities, please refer to the Microsoft website.

28.44. Exercise number 44

Type: Multimedia

Problem: Create a small piano with keys that sound when they are pressed.

Solution: To create and play a simple piano in Excel, you can generate a series of notes using Windows tones by pressing buttons. The *'sndPlaySound'* function of the Windows API can be used to play these notes. This exercise can be made more complex as desired.

Figure 104. Simple representation of three keys of a piano

A possible basic code would be the following: both the number of notes and the display of the keyboard could be improved and expanded. For instance, the keys could be colored to resemble those of a piano or programmed to produce sound when pressed on the computer keyboard.

The piano notes were obtained from a free online portal. Different internet webs offer free access to piano notes, allowing users to listen to and download them without charge. Alternatively, they could be recorded directly from a piano or other instrument.

```
Option Explicit
```

```
#If VBA7 Then
Private Declare PtrSafe Function sndPlaySound Lib "winmm.dll" Alias
"sndPlaySoundA" (ByVal lpszSoundName As String, ByVal uFlags As Long) As
Long
#Else
Private Declare Function sndPlaySound Lib "winmm.dll" Alias
"sndPlaySoundA" (ByVal lpszSoundName As String, ByVal uFlags As Long) As
Long
#End If
```

```
Private Sub A_Click()
    Call sndPlaySound("C:\Windows\Media\XXXX notaA.wav", 1)
End Sub
```

```
Private Sub B_Click()
    Call sndPlaySound("C:\Windows\Media\XXXX notaB.wav", 1)
End Sub
```

```
Private Sub C_Click()
    Call sndPlaySound("C:\Windows\Media\XXXX notaC.wav", 1)
End Sub
```

```
Private Sub D_Click()
    Call sndPlaySound("C:\Windows\Media\XXXX notaD.wav", 1)
End Sub
```

28.45. Exercise number 45

Type: Classes & Objects

Problem: Create a program that enables users to input the name of an animal species, its type, and the corresponding sound it makes into designated cells using a class module.

Solution: Excel offers default objects, such as an entire workbook, serving as a container for others like worksheets, each with their own properties and methods. Properties represent characteristics of the object, while methods denote actions that objects can perform. Although daily tasks often involve objects like sheets, rows, ranges, and columns, along with methods like 'delete', custom objects can also prove beneficial. This is achievable by employing a class module, facilitating the assignment of fully or partially custom properties and methods.

Given the aforementioned comment, to address this problem we start inserting a class module:

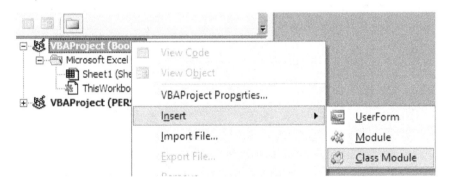

Figure 105. Creating a class module

Named: class_animal.

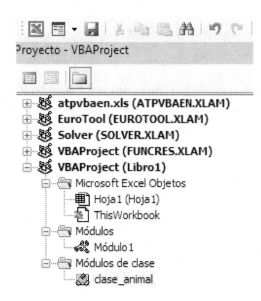

Figure 106. VBA project explorer

A routine must be created within this class module to record the names of animals, the respective sounds they make, and their classification as an insect, bird, fish, mammal, or reptile in the spreadsheet. Declare the following variables within the class module to accomplish this exercise:

```
Public name As String
Public specimen As String
Public sound As String
```

Then navigate to the spreadsheet and type the following heading:

	A	B	C
1	Name of animal	Type of animal	Sound
2			

Figure 107. Inserting headers in the first three columns

You can also rename the worksheet1 by animals:

Figure 108. Renaming a spreadsheet

To identify each empty row before inserting the recording, perform the following function. First, insert a button in the spreadsheet to make it easy to run the code from the sheet without going to the developer tab.

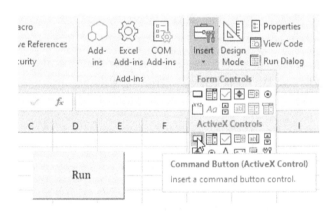

Figure 109. Inserting a form control

If you want, rename the button, and rename it "run":

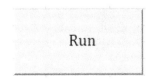

Figure 110. Button inserted using a form control

Finally, the program will ask for the name, type, and sound and place the information in the empty cells.

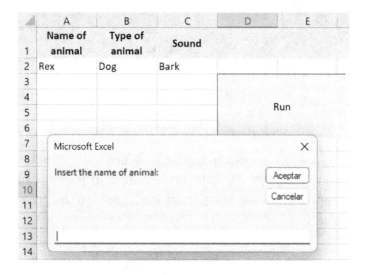

Figure 111. Insert Box

The code can be as follows. In the module:

```
Sub run()
Dim animal As New Class_Animal

  With animal

    .name = InputBox("Insert the name of animal: ")
    .sound = InputBox("Insert the sound of animal: ")
    .specimen = InputBox("Insert the species of animal: ")
    .newRegister 'Data will be written in a new row.

    'The registered data will now be written into cells

    ActiveCell.Offset(0, 0) = .name
    ActiveCell.Offset(0, 1) = .sound
    ActiveCell.Offset(0, 2) = .specimen

  End With
End Sub
```

And in the class module:

```
Public name As String
Public specimen As String
Public sound As String

Public Function newRegister()

        Worksheets("Animal").Range("A1").Select 'Initial location

        Do While ActiveCell <> Empty 'The loop will stop when data cell is
not empty

                ActiveCell.Offset(1, 0).Select

        Loop

End Function
```

28.46. Exercise number 46

Type: Classes & Objects

Problem: Write a program that inserts the name of a customer into the cells of a sheet, an amount, the total price including VAT and the date, so that this data is automatically inserted. The data must be requested via an "InputBox" window.

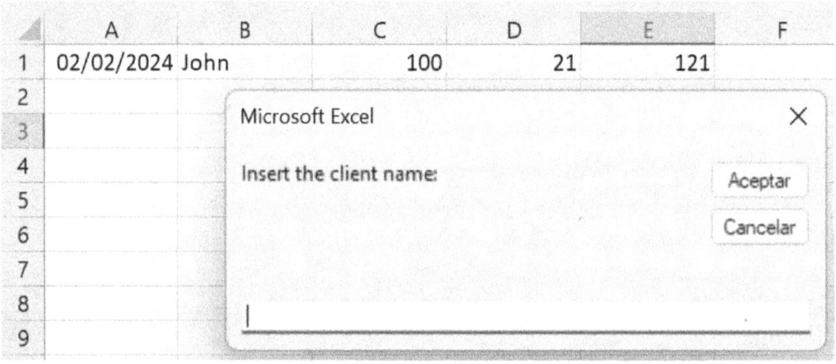

	A	B	C	D	E	F
1	02/02/2024	John	100	21	121	
2						
3			Microsoft Excel		✕	
4			Insert the client name:		Aceptar	
5						
6					Cancelar	
7						
8						
9						

Figure 112. Creating a class module

Solution: The problem can be solved in an analogous way to the previous example. To do this, place headings on the desired sheet. The program will then ask for the customer's name and the amount.

In the module:

```
Sub payment()

Dim client As New class_payment

  With client

      .dates = Date
      .name = InputBox("Insert the client's name: ")
      .cost = InputBox("Insert the cost: ")
      .vat = InputBox("Insert the value of vat: ")
      .newRegister 'Data will be written in a new row.

      'The registered data will now be written into cells

      ActiveCell.Offset(0, 0) = .dates
```

```
      ActiveCell.Offset(0, 1) = .name
      ActiveCell.Offset(0, 2) = .cost
      ActiveCell.Offset(0, 3) = .vat
      ActiveCell.Offset(0, 4) = .total


   End With
End Sub
```

Class Module:

```
Public name As String
Public cost As Double
Public dates As String
Public vat As Double
```

```
Public Function newRegister()

  Worksheets("Sheet1").Range("A1").Select 'Initial location

   Do While ActiveCell <> Empty 'The loop will stop when data cell is not
empty

        ActiveCell.Offset(1, 0).Select

   Loop

End Function
```

```
Public Function calculateVAT()

  calculateVAT = vat * cost / 100

End Function
```

```
Public Function total()

  total = calculateVAT + cost

End Function
```

28.47. Exercise number 47

Type: Classes & Objects

Problem: Insert an amount into a module so that the class module returns the amount for VAT. It is required to use the "Let" and "Get" properties.

Solution: To begin, create a class named *'VAT_Calculation'*.

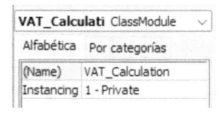

Figure 113. Renaming a class module

Select the class events 'initialize' and 'terminate'. An event is any action performed by a user on the interface that affects the program. In this case, when the class is initialized, the event is executed.

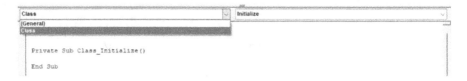

Within the class module code, declare variables in the 'Declarations' section at the top of the module. This ensures that they can be used in all subroutines (or methods) and properties throughout the class. It is important to note that these variables are private and only visible to the class.

Private vat_calculation As Double

Then, a "Get" and "Let" property procedure is inserted.

Figure 114. Inserting a new procedure

Then the next window will open. Give it a name, for example: "pricewithoutVAT" and click on Property:

Figure 115. Adding a new procedure with its properties

This procedure automatically generates the following lines, where 'as Variant' can be replaced with 'Double'. The data type 'as Variant' are for variables that are not explicitly stated and can contain any type of data except fixed-length string data. In other words, VBA provides a generic data type since it does not know the intended use, which can be changed later if necessary.

```
Public Property Get noVAT() As Double

End Property
```

```
Public Property Let noVAT(ByVal x As Double)

End Property
```

Properties are similar to variables as they store data values. The 'Calculation as Double' variable stores property values.

The preceding lines have been modified to suit our requirements. It is important to note that 'Get' is a read procedure, while 'Set' is a write procedure. These two procedures work in consonance, so the parameters sent must be consistent. For instance, if a double is sent, it is logical to receive a double. 'Get' and 'Let' are properties with the same name, and the 'Add Procedure' window facilitates this, preventing errors in property naming.

Insert the following code into the module by following the steps below:

1. The variables, including those of the new class type, will be declared.
2. Using the 'Set' command, assign the object instance to the new variable.

```
Option Explicit

Sub callClass()

    Dim result As Double
    Dim n As vat_calculation
    Set n = New vat_calculation

    n.noVAT = 5000
    result = n.final
    MsgBox result

End Sub
```

Following this, the statement *'Dim n As VAT calculation'* declares a variable named 'n' of type *'VAT calculation'*. This indicates that the variable 'n' can hold a reference to an object of the VAT calculation type.

The 'Set' statement is used to instantiate an object and assign it to a variable. In this instruction, 'Set n = New VAT calculation' instantiates the 'VAT calculation' class and assigns it to the variable 'n'. Following the execution of this statement, the variable 'n' holds a reference to the new instance of the 'VAT calculation' class.

Finally, the following code can be used in the class module:

```vba
Private vatVariable As Double


Private Sub Class_Initialize()

        MsgBox "There are a new class"

End Sub


Public Property Get noVAT() As Double

        noVAT = vatVariable

End Property


Public Property Let noVAT(ByVal x As Double)

        vatVariable = x

End Property


Public Property Get final() As Double

        final = noVAT * 1.21

End Property
```

The class module has not been headed or finished with the keyword 'class'. This is because the reserved keyword 'class' is not required in class modules.

Note:

The use of Get and Let properties in VBA depends on the specific design and functionality required in a program. These properties are useful for controlling the access to and the modification of variables in a class.

The Get property retrieves the value of a class variable, whereas the Let property assigns a value to a class variable. These properties can replace traditional public methods for reading and writing values to a class variable.

The use of these properties has the main advantage of enabling greater encapsulation of data within the class, thereby controlling access to the data, and preventing direct modification of the data from outside the class. Furthermore, the use of these properties can enhance code readability and comprehension.

However, it is important to note that overusing these properties can negatively impact program performance. The Get and Let properties result in additional function calls, so it is recommended to use them sparingly and evaluate their use based on the specific needs of each program.

28.48. Exercise number 48

Type: Classes & Objects

Problem: Color an active cell with any color, using a class module and module and the *Let* and *Get* properties. Define the Color in the module, using an index with which to Color the active cell.

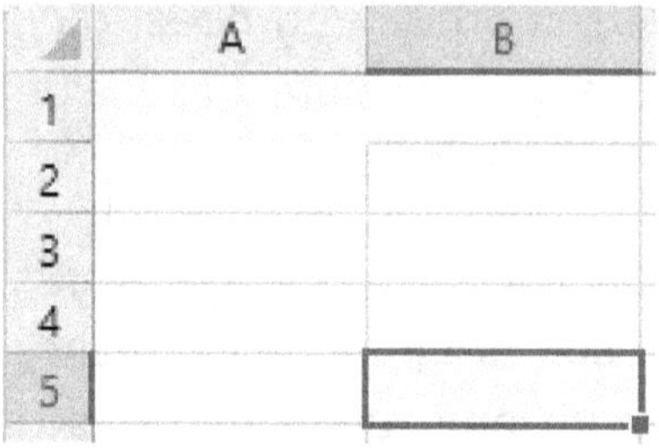

Figure 116. Example of filling an active cell

Solution: You can use the following code in the module:

```
Option Explicit


Sub paint()

    Dim index As paint
    Set index = New paint
    index.takeColour = 36
    ActiveCell.Interior.ColorIndex = index.finalColour

End Sub
```

In the class module, the code would be as follows:

```
Private color As Double

Public Property Get takeColour() As Double
        takeColour = color
End Property

Public Property Let takeColour(ByVal x As Double)
        color = x
End Property

Public Property Get finalColour() As Double
        finalColour = takeColour
End Property
```

28.49. Exercise number 49

Type: Classes & Objects

Problem: Perform a procedure using a class module that is used to sum two values in cell A1.

Solution: To solve this problem, create a procedure within a module to execute an object instance. In the class module, define the properties and methods. Type the following procedure in the module:

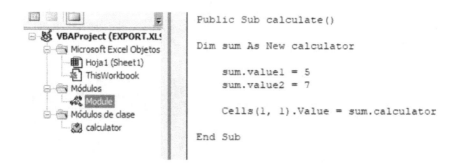

Figure 117. Adding two values using a class module

And in the class module, called "calculator", type the following code:

```
Option Explicit


Public value1 As Double
Public value2 As Double

Public Function calculator() As Double
    calculator = value1 + value2
End Function
```

For this problem, the data type 'double' has been chosen, although any other type could have been used. The result of the calculation, 5 + 7 = 12, will be displayed in cell A1.

28.50. Exercise number 50

Type: Classes & Objects

Problem: Perform a procedure using a class module that combines the first and last name of a client.

Solution: To solve this problem, create a procedure within a module to execute an object instance. Next, define the properties and methods within the class module. For instance, in the module, type the following procedure:

```
Option Explicit

Sub myModule()

        Dim myClient As New dsClient
        myClient.name = "John"
        myClient.surname = "Smith"
        MsgBox myClient.result

End Sub
```

In the class module, the following method:

```
Public name As String
Public surname As String

Public Function result() As String

  result = name & " " & surname

End Function
```

Figure 118. Class module to concatenate first and last name

28.51. Exercise number 51

Type: Classes & Objects

Problem: What are the differences between assigning an object-type variable and a string variable? Please provide an example.

Solution: There are significant differences between assigning an object-type variable and a string variable. These differences are not only due to the way they are assigned but also due to differences in concept:

1. Data type: Like other programming languages, VBA's object-type variable can store any type of object, including numbers, lists, dictionaries, and more. In contrast, a string variable can only store a single sequence of characters.
2. Operations: In VBA, object variables can perform specific operations based on the type of object they store, such as sorting or summing. However, string variables can only perform operations specific to strings, such as concatenation or substring search.
3. Mutability: Objects can be mutable or immutable. This means that some types of objects can be modified after they have been created, while others cannot. In VBA, strings are immutable, which means they cannot be modified once they have been created.
4. References: In VBA, when an object-type variable is assigned to another variable, both variables refer to the same object in memory. However, when a string variable is assigned to another variable, a copy of the original string is created.
5. Declaring variables: In VBA, it is important to declare variables before using them. Object-type variables are declared using the keyword 'Set', while string variables are declared using the keyword 'Dim'.

```
Sub object()

    Dim mySheet As Worksheet 'Assign variable of type object
    Dim myString As String ' Variable myString is type String
    Set mySheet = Application.ActiveSheet ' Variable mySheet is the active sheet
    myString = "Hello" 'Assign text to variable string
    ActiveSheet.Cells(1, 1).Value = mySheet.Name 'Cell A1 is equal to name of
active sheet

End Sub
```

In summary, when examining the previous example, it is important to note that 'mySheet' is an object of type WorkSheet with the property mySheet.name'. It is not possible to use myString.name with the string as it would result in an error.

Also, if you write sheet + "dot", i.e., sheet. the VBA will display the following image.

Figure 119. Accessing methods and properties with VBA

This object contains several methods and properties that can be accessed. However, "string" only accesses a specific property, which stores a text string.

28.52. Exercise number 52

Type: Classes & Objects

Problem: Using an array with three elements named 'One', 'Two', and 'Three', modify the value of 'One' to 'Four', following the approach of the previous exercise.

Solution: To solve this problem, declare and initialize an array of length 3 with the text string values 'One', 'Two', and 'Three'. Then, display the matrix values using the array index and the 'debug.print' statement.

```vba
Option Explicit


Sub mutability()

    'Declare and initialize the array
    Dim myArray(2) As String
    myArray(0) = "One"
    myArray(1) = "Two"
    myArray(2) = "Three"

    'Print data
    Debug.Print myArray(0)
    Debug.Print myArray(1)
    Debug.Print myArray(2)

    'Modify the data of some item in the array
    myArray(0) = "Four"

    'Print data again
    Debug.Print myArray(0)
    Debug.Print myArray(1)
    Debug.Print myArray(2)

End Sub
```

The first element of the array has been changed from 'One' to 'Four' using the array index. The modified values in the array are then displayed to confirm the change.

Note that modifying the value of an element in an array does not imply that text strings are mutable. The array only enables access to and modification of individual values within a text string.

28.53. Exercise number 53

Type: Classes & Objects

Problem: Assign an object variable to another object variable and compare the outcome when doing the same with a double variable of the same type.

Solution: This is a referencing problem. When an object variable is assigned to another variable, both variables refer to the same memory space. However, when you do the same with a variable of type Integer, Double, String, a copy of the original object is generated:

```
Option Explicit


Sub compare_variables()
    'Declare and assign a range object to object1
    Dim object1 As Range
    Set object1 = Range("A1")

    'Assign object1 to object2
    Dim object2 As Range
    Set object2 = object1

    'Declare and assign a double value to number1
    Dim number1 As Double
    number1 = 3.14

    'Assign number1 to number2
    Dim number2 As Double
    number2 = number1

    'Change the value of object2 to A2
    object2 = Range("A2")

    If object1 Is object2 Then
        MsgBox "The variables are the same"
        Else
            MsgBox "The variables are different"
    End If

    If number1 = number2 Then
        MsgBox "The variables double are the same"
```

```
        Else
            MsgBox "The variables double are different"
        End If

End Sub
```

Enter 25 and 3 into Range("A1") and Range("A2") respectively, as illustrated in the image below:

	A
1	25
2	3

Figure 120. Example of variable assignment

After running the macro, it is observed that the value of A1 changes from 25 to 3. However, the double maintains its original value.

A	B
3	3,14
3	2,71

Figure 121. Example of variable assignment

In the first scenario, the memory space remains the same. However, in the second scenario, the memory space differs, allowing independent updates of your data.

28.54. Exercise number 54

Type: Classes & Objects

Problem: Explain the diverse ways of creating an object or class instance.

Solution: This work has extensively covered the concept of classes and objects, which can be challenging to comprehend.

Objects are unequivocally linked to classes. Referring to objects created from a class is equivalent to referring to instances of classes. Additionally, variables and procedures are defined within classes. In VBA, classes are defined in class modules and class libraries.

When declaring a variable as an 'Object', it refers to a memory space located elsewhere, but not to the object itself. To properly assign an object, use the 'Set' statement. Object variables can be given an explicit class type or general types such as 'Variant' or 'Object'.

Using the word "new" *or using the* createObject *function generates a new class instance.*

Create an object variable for collections	
Dim myCollection As collection	Variable declaration of type Collection object
Set myCollection = New collection	Instance of the Collection object. Assigns the collection variable the reference to the object.
Dim myCollection As New collection	Combines variable declarations and creating the instance of type object
Another method for creating an object variable to store collections of key-value pairs.	
Dim myDictionary As Object	Declaration of Object Type Variable
Set myDictionary = CreateObject("Scripting.dictionary")	The Scripting.dictionary is an object that belongs to the Scripting object library.
Creating a variable object for spreadsheets	
Dim mySheet As Worksheet	Declaration of variable mySheet Type object
Set mySheet = ActiveSheet	Creating a variable object for active spreadsheets

Dim calculate As myClass	Declaration of the variable type object "myClass"
Set calculate = New myClass	Instance of the myClass object. Assigns the object reference to the calculation variable
Dim calculate As New myClass	Combine variable declarations and creating the object instance

Declarations of the type *'Dim Coll As New Collection'* are considered automatic instances or self-instances. However, the alternative method provides greater control over the object's lifespan. Auto instances can be instantiated with 'Set' equal to 'Nothing', but it cannot be determined if the object variable instantiates the object. Therefore, even though the variable is declared, it will not be instantiated until it is used for the first time.

28.55. Exercise number 55

Type: Macro Recording

Problem: Create a macro that types the word *'hello'* in an active cell and the word *'world'* in the adjacent cell.

Solution:

1. To begin, navigate to the 'Developer' tab on the ribbon and select the 'Record Macro' button located in the 'Code' group.

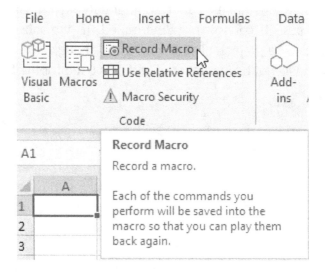

Figure 122. "Record Macro" icon

1. In the Record Macro dialogue box, type a name for the macro in the 'Macro Name' box, such as *'hello_world'*.

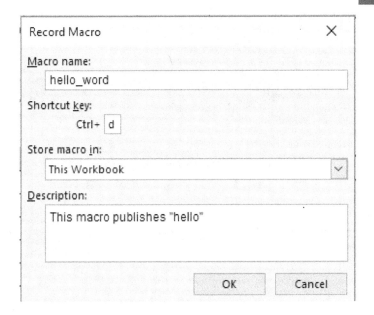

Figure 123. "Record Macro" dialog box

2. In the 'Shortcut key' box, you have the option to assign a key combination to quickly run the macro. If you choose not to assign a key combination, leave the box blank.
3. In the "Description" box, type a brief description about the macro's functionality if you wish. Otherwise, leave it blank.
4. In the "Save macro to" box, select "This workbook" if you only want the macro to be exclusive to this workbook. If you select "Personal Macro Workbook", the macro will be available in all workbooks.
5. Then, click the "OK" button to start recording the macro.
6. Perform the following actions: "Hello" in cell A1 and "World" in cell A2.
7. When you are finished, click the "Stop Recording" button in the same "Code" group of the "Developer" tab.

Figure 124. Button to stop macro recording

8. If desired, click the 'Run' button to execute the recorded macro. The output will resemble the following:

◢	A	B
1	hello	world

Figure 125. Macro recording example output

Finally, access the recorded code by clicking on the "Macros" button in the "Developer" tab.

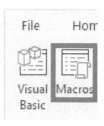

Figure 126. Macros button on the "Developer" tab

When this button is pressed, a list of all the macros available in the current workbook is displayed:

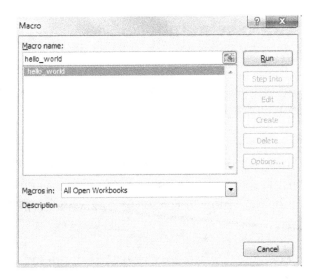

Figure 127. Accessing for the execution of a certain macro

Having clicked the 'Modify' button, the automatically recorded VBA code is as follows:

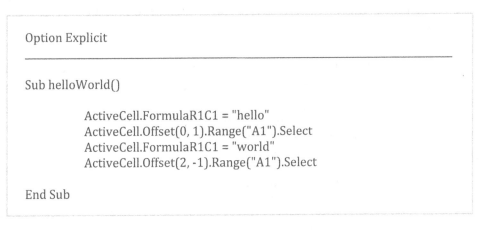

```
Option Explicit

Sub helloWorld()

        ActiveCell.FormulaR1C1 = "hello"
        ActiveCell.Offset(0, 1).Range("A1").Select
        ActiveCell.FormulaR1C1 = "world"
        ActiveCell.Offset(2, -1).Range("A1").Select

End Sub
```

This option is useful as it saves time and reduces errors. However, it is important to note that VBA will record every click, so it is recommended to practise the steps multiple times to avoid any unintended results.

28.56. Exercise number 56

Type: Events

Problem: Create a macro that automatically saves the contents of the sheet upon closing.

Solution: Events are actions that happen to an object, such as a sheet, workbook, button, or control, which can trigger code execution. They can be triggered by the user or the system and are used to perform a specific action in response to a change in the object's state.

For instance, the *'BeforeClose'* event is triggered immediately before an Excel workbook is closed. This event enables the user to execute specific VBA code before the workbook is closed.

Events are useful in Excel VBA as they allow for the automation of repetitive or complex tasks and improve user interactivity with the application. Macros can be created using events to automatically respond to user actions, saving time and reducing errors when working with data in Excel.

Throughout my career, I have used many events. To view all of them, please go to ThisWorkbook.

Figure 128. Accessing the modules of a book

Then, expand the list of events:

Figure 129. List of events

As you can see, there are a lot of them. In this case, select "Before Close" and add the following line:

```
Private Sub Workbook_BeforeClose(cancel as Boolean)

        ThisWorkbook.Save

End Sub
```

You should check that the code works by closing the workbook, which will prompt it to be saved.

28.57. Exercise number 57

Type: Events

Problem: Make a macro run by double-clicking on an active cell, within the "A:A" range. The macro should count the number of active sheets, by pressing a button, list them in column "A" and when clicking on one of them it will go to the corresponding sheet.

	A	B	C
1	Sheet1		
2	Sheet2		
3	Sheet3	Counter	
4	Sheet4		
5	Sheet5		
6	Sheet6		
7	Sheet7		
8	Sheet8		

Figure 130. Sheet counting exercise

Solution: This macro is developed for "sheet1" with the "BeforeDoubleClick" event.

Figure 131. "BeforeDoubleClick" Instruction in Sheet 1

This feature enables an action to be performed by double-clicking a cell. However, to count the number of sheets, a separate procedure will be required.

```
Option Explicit
```

```
Private Sub worksheet_beforeDoubleClick(ByVal target As Range, cancel As
Boolean)

    Dim myRange As String
    myRange = "A:A"

    If Not Application.Intersect(Range(myRange), target) Is Nothing Then
        If target.Value <> "" Then
            Sheets(target.Value).Select
        End If
    End If

End Sub
```

```
Public Sub counterSheets()

    Dim i As Integer
    Dim c As Integer

    Sheet1.Range("A:A").ClearContents
    c = 1

      For i = 1 To Sheets.Count
        Sheet1.Cells(c, 1).Value = Sheets(i).Name
        c = c + 1
      Next

End Sub
```

The BeforeDoubleClick prevents the cell layout from opening. In other words, this event does not allow you to write inside the cell, because all you want is for it to go to the indicated sheet. Then, you only want this event to be available within a certain range, but if the cell is not empty, and you click on it.

28.58. Exercise number 58

Type: Skills

Problem: Send one or more simple emails from Excel, including the sender, recipient, CC, BCC, subject, and message body.

	A	B
1	From	vbaExcel@hotmail.com
2	To	dearReader@gmail.com
3	CC	
4	BBC	
5	Subject	Concept Test
6	Body	Try to send an email from Excel

Table 15. Sender, recipient, CC, CO, subject & message body

Solution: It is possible to send emails through a configured Outlook account using Excel and VBA. To achieve this, the following references are required:

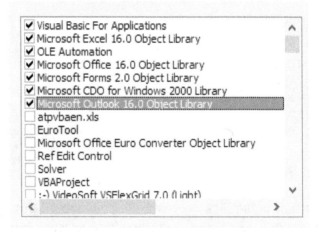

Figure 132. References needed to send emails

Then, insert a new module named "email" and use a public procedure.

```vba
Option Explicit


Public Sub sendEmail()

        Dim App As Object
        Dim email As Object
        Set App = CreateObject("outlook.application")
        App.Session.Logon
        Set email = App.CreateITem(0)

        With email

                .SentOnBehalfOfName = Sheet1.Cells(1, 2).Value
                .To = Sheet1.Cells(2, 2).Value
                .CC = Sheet1.Cells(3, 2).Value
                .BCC = Sheet1.Cells(4, 2).Value
                .Subject = Sheet1.Cells(5, 2).Value
                .Body = Sheet1.Cells(6, 2).Value

                'Send automatic
                .Send
        End With

        Set email = Nothing
        Set App = Nothing

End Sub
```

28.59. Exercise number 59

Type: Error Handling

Problem: Generate an error by dividing 10 by 0 so that the program continues to run, even if the error occurs.

```
Option Explicit

Sub handle_Errors()

On Error GoTo handleErrors

    ' Error Example:
    Dim divider As Integer
    divider = 0
    Dim result As Integer
    result = 175 / divider

    ' Continue with the code if there are no errors

    MsgBox "Result: " & result

    Exit Sub

handleErrors:

    'handle Errors

    MsgBox "Error " & Err.Number & ": " & Err.Description

End Sub
```

In the previous exercise, the 'On Error GoTo' statement was used, followed by a label (in this case, 'HandleError') to indicate where to go in case of error. If an error occurs during code execution, VBA will automatically jump to the specified tag. Then, under the 'HandleError' label, code can be added to manage the error, such as displaying an error message, undoing changes, closing files, or taking any other necessary action.

The 'On Error' statement should be used cautiously and only to manage specific, known errors. It is crucial to ensure that the code is robust and has proper error handling to prevent unnoticed errors from causing problems to the application.

28.60. Exercise number 60

Type: Error Handling

Problem: Generate an error by dividing 10 by 0 so that the program continues to run, even if an error occurs. Use the statement: "On Error Resume Next" and "On Error GoTo 0".

Solution: Dividing any number by 0 will always produce an indeterminacy (error), resulting in an error of 11 at runtime. To avoid this error, the program can be instructed to skip such an erroneous instruction through error handling.

```
Option Explicit


Sub handlingErrorResumeNext()

    'Example of error
    Dim divider As Integer
    Dim result As Integer
    divider = 0

    'We use On Error Resume Next to continue execution
    'even though an error occurs:
    On Error Resume Next
    result = 10 / divider

    'We check if an error occurred
    If Err.Number <> 0 Then

        'Error handling
        MsgBox "Error " & Err.Number & ": " & Err.Description
        'You can add additional code to handle how to undo: uploads, close: files,
        'Then you can reset the error handler with the "On Error GOTO 0"
statement
        On Error GoTo 0
        Exit Sub

    End If
    'We reset the error handler
    On Error GoTo 0
    'Continue with the code if there are no errors
    MsgBox "Result: " & result
```

End Sub

In this exercise, the code uses the 'On Error Resume Next' statement to continue running despite any errors. The 'if' statement then checks for errors using the 'Err.Number' property. If an error is found, the code displays a message and performs the necessary actions as requested by the user. Finally, the error handler is reset using the 'On Error GoTo 0' statement to ensure that subsequent errors are managed normally.

The 'On Error GoTo 0' statement in VBA for Excel resets error handling to its default state. This means that any previous error handling configured using 'On Error GoTo [tag]' or 'On Error Resume Next' is disabled.

It is important to exercise caution when using 'On Error Resume Next' as it can obscure bugs and hinder the detection and resolution of issues in your code. It is advisable to use this method only when it is certain that error handling in this way is appropriate and safe for your application. Proper error handling is crucial to ensure the reliability and robustness of the code.

28.61. Exercise number 61

Type: Error Handling

Problem: Use the *"Static"* statement to update a counter that indicates the number of times a macro run. That is, make a counter that counts the number of times you click the *"play"* button that runs the macro.

Option Explicit

Sub counter()

    ' Declaration of Static Variable
    Static counter As Integer

    ' Initialization of counter in first running
    If counter= 0 Then
        counter = 1
    End if

    ' Showing the actual value of counter
    MsgBox "Counter: " & counter

    ' Increase the counter number
    counter = counter + 1

End Sub

To complete this exercise, declare a variable named 'counter' as 'Static' to maintain its value between different runs of the macro. Set the counter value to 1 on the first run. Display the current value of the counter in a message box using the MsgBox function and increase it by 1 with each subsequent run of the macro.

If the variable had been declared as "dim", the counter would have been useless because in each execution the initial value would be 1. Take the test, changing "Static" to "Dim".

Declaring a variable as "Static" in VBA can be useful when you need to maintain the value of a variable between different runs of a macro, share information between different procedures in the same module, or avoid restarting a variable at each call to a procedure.

28.62. Exercise number 62

Type: Variables, Constants, and Types

Problem: Write code that displays the results of various comparisons with a variable named 'empty', which is declared as a Variant type. The results should be shown through pop-up messages (MsgBox). The comparisons include:

- Show "True" if the "empty" variable is empty using the IsEmpty function.
- Show "True" if the "empty" variable equals False.
- Show "True" if the variable "empty" equals an empty string ("").
- Show "True" if the variable "empty" is equal to zero (0).

After making such comparisons, assign the Empty value directly to the "*empty*" variable.

Solution: The 'Variant' data type can store any type of data except for fixed-length strings and user-defined types. Additionally, 'Variant' can store special values of type 'Empty', 'Null', 'Missing', 'Nothing', and 'Error'.

Upon declaration, the 'Variant' variable defaults to 'empty', which can be interpreted as a zero, zero-length string, or false depending on the context. To determine if a variable is 'empty', use the 'IsEmpty' statement.

```vba
Option Explicit

Sub emptyVariable()

        Dim variableEmpty As Variant

        ' Show if the variable 'empty' is empty using IsEmpty
        MsgBox IsEmpty(variableEmpty)

        ' Show if variable 'empty' is equal to False
        MsgBox variableEmpty = False

        ' Show if the variable 'empty' is equal to an empty string ("")
        MsgBox variableEmpty = ""

        ' Show if the variable 'empty' is equal to zero (0)
        MsgBox variableEmpty = 0

        ' Empty can be assigned directly to a Variant Variable
        variableEmpty = Empty

End Sub
```

Note: A fixed-length string is a data type with a predetermined size that is set at the time of declaration and remains constant throughout program execution. A fixed-length string is a data type with a predetermined size that is set at the time of declaration and remains constant throughout program execution. It cannot be dynamically changed.

28.63. Exercise number 63

Type: Variables, Constants, and Types

Problem: Create a VBA macro in Excel named 'NullVariable' that checks whether a Variant variable named 'null' is null or not. The macro should assign null to the 'null' variable and then use the 'IsNull' function to determine if the variable is null. If the variable is null, a warning message should be displayed stating 'Variant variable is null'. If the variable is not null, a message should be displayed stating 'Variant variable is NOT null'.

Solution: At this point, you may be wondering about the difference between an 'empty' and 'null' variable. In VBA, the main distinction is that an empty variable has no valid value assigned to it and its value is indeterminate, whereas a null variable explicitly has the null value, indicating the absence of any value or data in the variable.

```
Option Explicit
_____

Public Sub nullVariable()

Dim variableNull As Variant
variableNull = Null

            If IsNull(variableNull) Then
                    MsgBox "Variable Variant is Null"
                        Else
                                MsgBox "Variable Variant is NOT
Null"
                End if

End Sub
```

In the previous exercise, the variable 'empty' was declared, but nothing was assigned to it. It is important to note that an Empty variable differs from an empty string (") or a numeric value of zero (0).

A Null variable is a variable that has been assigned specifically to the value Null, as in this exercise. The term 'Null' indicates the absence of any value or data in the variable. Null variables are of a special type and are primarily used in the context of databases to indicate the lack of a value in a record field.

28.64. Exercise number 64

Type: Variables, Constants, and Types

Problem: Create a procedure in Excel VBA named 'text' with an optional parameter named 'parameters'. The purpose of this macro is to display a message in a dialog box based on whether a value is provided for the 'parameters' parameter. To ensure proper handling of cases where a value is or is not provided for the optional parameter, use the 'isMissing' function.

Solution: The "IsMissing" function determines whether an argument has been passed to an optional parameter of type Variant.

```
Option Explicit


Public Sub missing()

        text  ' Try without arguments
        ' text ("my argument") ' Try with arguments

End Sub


Public Sub text (optional parameters As Variant)

        If IsMissing(parameters) Then
                MsgBox "There are not parameters"
                    Else
                            MsgBox " There are parameters "
        End if

End Sub
```

28.65. Exercise number 65

Type: Variables, Constants, and Types

Problem: Determine the type of variable at run time. To do this, first declare a variable and then use the *typeName* and *VarType functions*, determine the type of variable.

Solution: *TypeName* is a function that returns a text string representing the data type of a variable at runtime. This can be useful in situations where the data type of a variable is unknown in advance or when performing a kind of check at runtime.

VarType is a function that returns a numeric value representing the data type of a variable or expression. The value 2 corresponds to vbInteger. A complete list of values can be found on Microsoft's VBA website, including vbEmpty = 0, vbNull = 1, etc.

```
Option Explicit


Public Sub typeinRunningTime()

Dim c As Integer

MsgBox TypeName(c)

        If VarType(c) = vbInteger Then ' vbInteger = 2
                MsgBox "c is an Integer"
                Else
                MsgBox "c is NOT an Integer"
        End if

End Sub
```

28.66. Exercise number 66

Type: Variables, Constants, and Types

Problem: Convert a variable of type double into a monetary value placed in a cell of a worksheet, then convert this variable to an integer variable without decimals.

Solution: There are various methods of data conversion, which involve converting one type of data into another. Examples include CBool, CByte, and CInt. These functions have been used to solve various problems, such as adding days to a date that has been edited as a string. In some cases, it may be necessary to represent a numeric value in a monetary format within a cell.

```
Option Explicit


Public Sub conversions()

        Dim myDecimal As Double
        Dim myInteger as Integer
        Dim M As Currency 'variable monetary

        myDecimal = 1113.259
        M = CCur(myDecimal)

        Sheet1.Range( "A1").Value = M
        myInteger = CInt (myDecimal)
        Sheet1.Range("A2").Value = myInteger

End Sub
```

Finally, it is worth noting that a decimal value can be converted to an integer using the *CInt* function. This function truncates the decimals and converts the numerical value to an integer. It is important to keep in mind that decimals are truncated and not rounded when using the *CInt* function. Therefore, if rounding is required before converting to a whole number, other rounding functions such as *Round* should be employed.

28.67. Exercise number 67

Type: Variables, Constants, and Types

Problem: Calculate the volume of a cylinder, using the following constants, Radius = 5 units, height = 10 units. Then, try changing the height.

Solution: To perform this exercise, remember that the volume of a straight cylinder is the area of the base times the height (h), i.e., $V = \pi \cdot R^2 \cdot h$. Remember that PI is approximately 3.14159...

```
Sub constants()

    Const pi As Double = 3.14159
    Const radius As Double = 5
    Const height As Double = 10

    'Calculate the volume of a cylinder using the following constants:
    Dim volume As Double
    volume = pi * (radius ^ 2) * height

    'Display the result
    MsgBox "Volume cylinder is: " & volume

    'This instruction will give an error because you cannot change the value of
one constant
    'height = 20
    'volume = pi * (radius ^ 2) * height

    'Display the result
    'MsgBox "The new volume of cylinder is:" & volume

End Sub
```

The main difference between a variable declared as constant and one declared as "*dim*" in VBA is that constants have a fixed value that cannot be changed once a value is assigned. However, variables of type "*dim*" can change their value during code execution. For this reason, it is possible to perform autoincrements of the type i = i + 1 or c = c * 5. If "i", "c" or another variable were declared as constant, it would be impossible to perform an autoincremental.

Finally, if you declare the height variable as 'dim', you can change the height of the cylinder as many times as needed.

This is a common feature in modern object-oriented programming languages.

28.68. Exercise number 68

Type: Variables, Constants, and Types

Problem: Create a user-defined function to produce all existing values in a selected range of cells. If the selection contains only one number or the product of numeric values is made by non-numeric values, use the "isError" and "CVerr" functions.

Solution: The *CVerr* function can be used to assign errors to variables of type Variant. This is particularly useful for returning errors from user-defined functions in Excel sheets. To check if the variable is storing any errors, use the *IsError* function.

The following code can be used by inserting it into a module.

```
Option Explicit


Public Function productValues (numbers As Variant) As Variant

Dim number As Variant
number = 1
productValues = 1

            If Not IsArray (numbers) Then
                    productValues = CVErr(2015) '#Value!
                    Exit Function
            End If

            For Each number In numbers
                    productValues = productValues * number
            Next number

End Function
```

The CVErr(2015) bug is a type of bug related to user-defined roles. This error occurs when a user-defined function returns the error "#VALUE!" or "#VALOR!" instead of the expected numeric or other value. This happens when the calculations are incorrect, for example, 12 multiplied by 'a' or 25 multiplied by zero.

28.69. Exercise number 69

Type: Variables, Constants, and Types

Problem: Perform a procedure that sends a valid object and another object of type 'nothing' to another procedure. The receiving procedure must check if the object is valid and of the 'nothing' type using 'IsObject' and 'Is Nothing'.

Solution: In VBA, you cannot directly assign a "null" to an object. However, you can get a similar result by using the keyword, "nothing" which allows you to represent the absence of an object. It is important to note that after assigning "nothing" to an object, no property or method of the object can be accessed until a new reference is assigned to a valid object. This problem is interesting in terms of professional development because when trying to access a null object, it can generate runtime errors. So, it is a good practice to check if an object is of the "nothing" type before trying to access its methods and properties.

Try the following code in your editor. Uncomment a few lines of code and see what happens.

```vba
Option Explicit


Sub sendArgument()
    'Dim myObjet As Object 'The process begins with the declaration of an object.
    'Set myObjet = sheetl.Range("A:A") 'The assignment is designated as rank A:A.
    'Set myObject = Nothing 'Then, an attempt is made to assign a null value.

    Dim myObject As String 'Attempting to declare the object as a string to observe the outcome.
    myObject = "Hello!" 'A text string is assigned an object.

    reciveParameter myObject 'The object argument is sent.
End Sub
```

```vba
Public Sub reciveParameter(myParameter As Variant)
    If IsObject(myParameter) Then
    MsgBox "The parameter is an object"
        If myParameter Is Nothing Then
            MsgBox "The parameter is an empty object"
            End If
                Else
                MsgBox "The parameter is not an object"
    End If
End Sub
```

28.70. Exercise number 70

Type: Variables, Constants, and Types

Problem: Create two procedures: one main procedure with no parameters and another parameterized procedure. The main procedure should send arrays of type 'Variant' that are declared as simple, dynamic, and fixed. The parameterized procedure should receive the array, verify that it is parameterized using the 'isArray' function, and then display each of the received parameters in a pop-up window.

Solution: Arrays can be declared with a specific data type, such as an integer or a double. When declaring procedures with parameters, it is important to declare them as the appropriate variable type. In this case, the array will be declared as a Variant, meaning that the arguments will be of the same type. This is necessary because the problem statement requires the use of the isArray function, which checks whether a Variant object is storing an array.

This problem involves four types of variables. The first type is a simple statement, such as *'dim arrangement as Variant'*. The second type is a declaration of a variable in the form of a dynamic array, which is achieved by using empty parentheses, i.e., *'dim array() as Variant'*. The third type is a fixed-length array declared with a non-empty parenthesis, such as *'dim array(3) as Variant'*. The arrangement will have four elements because VBA starts counting from zero (0, 1, 2, 3). Finally, declaring a text string as such can lead to explicit error generation.

```vba
Option Explicit
```

```vba
Public Sub arraysWithVariants()

    'An array of type Variant is generated.
    Dim myArray As Variant 'This is a simple variable declaration that can hold
any type of data.
    myArray = Array(1, 2, 3)
    printArray myArray

    'An array of type Variant is generated.
    Dim variantArray() As Variant 'This is a dynamic array of non-fixed
dimensions.
    variantArray = Array(4, 5, 6)
    printArray variantArray

    'An array of type String.
    Dim stringArray(2) As String 'This is a fixed-size static array.
    stringArray(0) = "A"
    stringArray(1) = "B"
    stringArray(2) = "C"
    printArray stringArray

    'A variable to generate an error.
    Dim generateError As String 'This is a string variable created specifically to
generate an error.
    generateError = "ERROR"
    printArray generateError

End Sub
```

```vba
Public Sub printArray(myArray As Variant)
    Dim c As Long

    If Not IsArray(myArray) Then 'If not is a logical operator that negates the
result of isArray(arr).
                'If Arr is not an array, this statement will be true.
        Err.Raise 5 'This instruction intentionally creates an error during
execution with error number_ five.
                'The number five is the argument that allows the generation of this
error.
    End If

    For c = LBound(myArray) To UBound(myArray)
```

```
        MsgBox myArray(c)
    Next c

End Sub
```

28.71. Exercise number 71

Type: Variables, Constants, and Types

Problem: Define a new data type named 'employee' with three properties: Name, Age, and Salary. Assign a name to each property and display them in a message box.

Solution: User-defined types (UDTs) enable the creation of custom objects without the need to create a class module. The difference between the two is that the class module allows for the creation of custom properties and methods, while the UDT only allows for custom properties. However, sometimes custom properties are all that is required. The UDT is declared with a 'Type' and 'End Type' statement, which can be of the Public or Private type.

```
'Firstly, we define the data type, always outside of any procedure

Type Employee
   Name As String
   Age As String
   Salary As Double
End Type
```

```
Sub exampleUDT()

   Dim myEmployee As Employee
   myEmployee.Name = "John"
   myEmployee.Age = 30
   myEmployee.Salary = 1510.25

   MsgBox "Employee Name: " & myEmployee.Name
   MsgBox " Employee Age: " & myEmployee.Age
   MsgBox " Employee Salary: " & myEmployee.Salary

End Sub
```

28.72. Exercise number 72

Type: Variables, Constants, and Types

Problem: Define a new data type for representing imaginary numbers. Then, perform addition and multiplication operations on two imaginary numbers.

Solution: An imaginary number is a mathematical concept represented by a combination of a real number 'a' and an imaginary unit 'b', in the form 'a + bi'. Imaginary numbers were first introduced to solve second-degree equations where square roots of negative numbers appeared. Imaginary numbers are used in various areas of mathematics and physics, including the theory of electrical circuits, quantum mechanics, the theory of complex functions, and a wide variety of technical fields. The extension of complex numbers is known as quaternions. This concept is applied, for example, to the control of drones, planes, rockets, ships, and objects that use gyroscopes and accelerometers.

```vba
Option Explicit


Type imaginariumNumber
   realPart As Double
   imaginariumPart As Double
End Type


Sub myImaginariumNumbers()
Dim z1 As imaginariumNumber
Dim z2 As imaginariumNumber
Dim sum As imaginariumNumber
Dim product As imaginariumNumber

z1.realPart = 1
z1.imaginariumPart = 2

z2.realPart = 3
z2.imaginariumPart = 4
```

```
'product: z1 = a + bi y z2 = c + di = (a·c – b·d) + (a·d + b·c)i --> (1 + 2i)*(3 + 4i)
= 1·3 + 1·4i + 2·3i -2*4 = - 5 +10i

product.realPart = z1.realPart * z2.realPart - z1.imaginariumPart *
z2.imaginariumPart
product.imaginariumPart = z1.realPart * z2.imaginariumPart +
z1.imaginariumPart * z2.realPart

'sum: z1 = a + bi y z2 = c + di = (a + c) + (b + d)i
sum.realPart = z1.realPart + z2.realPart
sum.imaginariumPart = z1.imaginariumPart + z2.imaginariumPart

MsgBox "z1 = " & z1.realPart & " + " & z1.imaginariumPart & "i" & vbCrLf & _
    "z2 = " & z2.realPart & " + " & z2.imaginariumPart & "i" & vbCrLf & _
    "z1 + Z2 = " & sum.realPart & " + " & sum.imaginariumPart & "i" & vbCrLf
& _
    "z1 * Z2 = " & product.realPart & " + " & product.imaginariumPart & "i"

End Sub
```

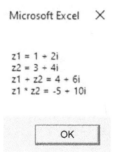

Figure 133. Dialog box showing the result

28.73. Exercise number 73

Type: Variables, Constants, and Types

Problem: Use an "*enum*" to select one of four options and display that option in a dialog box of type "MsgBox".

Solution: An enumeration is a predefined list of options or values that can be represented in text or numerical form. It improves the readability of the code, makes the code easier to maintain and generates "self-documentation" of the code.

```
Option Explicit
```

```
Enum options

    Option1 = 1
    option2 = 2
    option3 = 3
    option4 = 4

End Enum
```

```
Sub problemEnum()
Dim selection As options

MsgBox ("Select an option: " & vbCrLf & "1. Option 1" & vbCrLf & "2. Option 2"
& vbCrLf & "3. Option 3" & vbCrLf & "4. Option 4")

selection = InputBox("Insert an option: ")

        Select Case selection

                Case Option1
                MsgBox "Has choose the first option: "

                Case option2
                MsgBox " as choose the second option: "

                Case option3
                MsgBox "Has choose the third option: "
```

```
                Case option4
                MsgBox "Has choose the fourth option: "

        End Select
End Sub
```

This exercise involves defining an enumeration named 'options' that comprises of four elements: option1, option2, option3, and option4, each with an associated numeric value. The InputBox function is then used to input one of the four options, which is recorded in 'choice'. A 'Select Case' structure is then used to evaluate the user's choice and display a corresponding message with the selected option.

28.74. Exercise number 74

Type: Collections & Arrays

Problem: Create a collection that adds any four items, counts them, deletes the second item, extracts any item from the collection, and finally, cleans up the collection.

Solution: The *Collection* object stores a collection of items in a specific order. It can store any type of data and objects except user-defined types. Collections start at index 1, unlike arrays that start at index 0 by default. The *Collection* object is designed to be simple and easy to use, with a small set of methods that allow you to *add*, *remove, count,* and *recover*. Therefore, collections have four simple methods: Add, Remove, Count, and Item. The last one is the Collection class's default method allows retrieval of an item with a specific index without the need for explicit writing. To delete a collection, assign the collection to a new collection.

Finally, it is important to note that items in a collection cannot be reassigned once they have been defined. While objects in a collection can be mutated, the object reference variable cannot be reassigned.

```vb
Option Explicit


Public Sub collections()

        ' New Collection
        Dim collections As Collection
        Set collections = New Collection

        ' We add the elements of the collection with the with
        With collections
                .Add  "first"
                .Add "second"
                .Add "third"
```

```vb
                    .Add "forty"
        End With

        ' We count the elements
        MsgBox "The number of elements is: " & collections.Count

        ' We delete any element
        collections.Remove 2

        ' Read the data of an element
        MsgBox " Give me number two of the collection:  " & collections(2)
        MsgBox " Give me number two of the collection:  " &
collections.Item(2)


        'We cannot reassign a collection element
        ' collections(4) = "New data" ' Generates an error

        ' Clean the whole collection
        Set collections = New Collection

        'MsgBox " Give me number two of the collection: " & collections(2)
'it Will give an error.

        'because it is empty

        collections.Add "A", "Hello"
        MsgBox " The new collection item is: " & collection(1)

End Sub
```

28.75. Exercise number 75

Type: Collections & Arrays

Problem: Repeat the same problem as above but using the key-value relationship.

Solution: Items in a collection can be accessed through their index or key, which consists of a unique piece of information assigned to each item.

```
Option Explicit

Public Sub collections()

        ' New Collection

        Dim collections As Collection
        Set collections = New Collection

        ' We add the elements of the collection with the with

        With collections
                .Add 1, "Key_1"
                .Add 2, "Key_2"
                .Add 3, "Key_3"
                .Add 4, "Key_4"
        End With

        ' We count the elements
        MsgBox "The number of elements is: " & collections.Count

        ' We delete any element
        collections.Remove 2

        ' We read the data of an element
        MsgBox " Give me number two of the collection:  " & collections(2)
        MsgBox " Give me number two of the collection:  " &
collections.Item(2)
        MsgBox " Give me number three of the collection: " &
collections("key 3")

        'We cannot reassign a collection element
```

```vba
' collections(4) = "New data"
' Generates an error

'We clean the whole collection
Set collections = New Collection

'MsgBox " Give me number two of the collection: " & collections(2)
'it Will give an error.

'because it is empty

collections.Add "A", "Hello"
MsgBox " The new collection item is: " & collection(1)
MsgBox " The new collection item is: " & collection("Hello!")

End Sub
```

28.76. Exercise number 76

Type: Collections & Arrays

Problem: Use a *"for"* loop to cycle through all items in a collection, and when a match exists, display a message in a pop-up window.

Solution: To efficiently iterate over a collection, it is useful to use the 'for each' loop, although other types of loops are also possible.

```
Option Explicit


Public Sub collections ( )

        Dim c As Variant
        Dim collections As Collection
        Set collections = New Collection

        collections.Add 1
        collections.Add 2
        collections.Add 3
        collections.Add 4

        For Each c In collections

                If c = 1 Then
                        MsgBox "Hola Mundo!"
                End If
        Next c
End sub
```

28.77. Exercise number 77

Type: Collections & Arrays

Problem: Create a non-uniform collection consisting of four sub-collections with varying numbers of items. Additionally, print the fourth element of the second sub-collection.

Solution: In Excel VBA, a *Jagged Collection* is a collection of collections that can contain a variable number of items. This concept is simpler to understand than it seems.

```vba
Option Explicit


Public Sub irregularCollection ()

        Dim specimenMammal As New Collection
        Dim specimenReptile As New Collection
        Dim specimenBird As New Collection
        Dim specimenAnimal As New Collection
        Dim irregularCollection As New Collection

        specimenMammal.Add "Dog" ' First Collection
        specimenReptile.Add "Chameleon" ' Second Collection
        specimenBird.Add "Flamingo" ' Third Collection

        specimenAnimal.Add "Dog" ' Forty Collection, first element
        specimenAnimal.Add "Chameleon" ' Forty Collection, second
element
        specimenAnimal.Add "Flamingo" ' Forty Collection, third element

        irregularCollection.Add specimenMammal ' Fifty Collection, first
element
        irregularCollection.Add specimenReptile  ' Fifty Collection, second
element
        irregularCollection.Add specimenBird ' Fifty Collection, third
element
        irregularCollection.Add specimenAnimal ' Fifty Collection, forty
element
        MsgBox irregularCollection (4) (2) 'it will print item 4 o 2º
collection
End Sub
```

28.78. Exercise number 78

Type: Collections & Arrays

Problem: Create a class named '*clsAnimal*' that displays the name, species, and superspecies of an animal collection. The collection should be defined in the standard module, and the class module should show the data for that collection.

Solutions: Collections are a useful solution for storing objects, including instances of user-defined classes, making it easier to store and manipulate data in VBA.

Class instances can also be added to a collection, in addition to strings or values. To do so, follow this solution:

```
Option Explicit


'Standard Module: Animal Collection
Public Sub collectionAnimal ()

        Dim AnimalCollection As New Collection
        Dim A As clsAnimal

        'Add new animal
        Set = A New clsAnimal
        A.name = "Dog"
        A. Specimen = "mammal"
        A.super_ Specimen = "Canis lupus familiaris"
        AnimalCollection.Add A

        'Add new animal
        Set = A New clsAnimal
        A.name = "Pigeon"
        A. Specimen = "bird"
        A.super_ Specimen = "Columbidae"
        AnimalCollection.Add A

        'Add new animal
        Set = A New clsAnimal
        A.name = "Iguana"
        A. Specimen = "Reptile"
```

```
            A.super_ Specimen = "Iguanidae"
            AnimalCollection.Add A

            'Print all item data
            For Each In AnimalCollection
                        A.print
            Next A

            'Remove all item data
            Set AnimalCollection = Nothing

End Sub
```

```
Option Explicit
_____

' Class module named clsAnimal

Public Name As String
Public Specimen As String
Public super_specimen

Public Sub print ( )

        MsgBox Name & "it is member of: " & Specimen & "at the same
time of:" super_specimen

End sub
```

28.79. Exercise number 79

Type: Collections & Arrays

Problem: Perform an exercise in which a list of people's names is stored in a VBA-Excel collection, and then iterate through the collection to display those names in a message window. Additionally, retrieve and delete an item from the collection using the key and display the number of items remaining in the collection after deletion.

Solution: A VBA collection is a dynamic data structure used to store and organize items. It is like an array in other programming languages, but with the added benefit of being able to change size during code execution.

In a collection, items are stored in a list and identified by keys or indexes. Each element can be of any data type, such as numbers, text strings, dates, objects, or other data elements. Collections in VBA are objects in the Collection class, which provides methods and properties for adding, deleting, searching, and manipulating items in the collection.

Collections are useful for automating processes in Excel. For example, they can be used to store a dynamic list of values obtained from a spreadsheet, to organize objects such as ranges of cells or graphs, or to store and manage data in a flexible, easy-to-use data structure in VBA code. Collections are a powerful tool for working with dynamic datasets and provide flexibility in data manipulation in automated Excel applications.

In a collection, each item is added using the 'Add' method and associated with a unique key. The syntax for adding an item to a collection is as follows:

myCollection.Add Item, Key

Where *"myCollection"* refers the name of the collection, *"Item"* refers to the value or object you want to add, and *"Key"* is the unique identifier for the item in the collection.

The value of 'Item1' can be retrieved from the collection at any time by using the key: 'Key1': *element = myCollection("Key1")*

With all the above, the exercise could be solved as follows:

```vb
Option Explicit
```

```vb
Sub collectionExample( )

        ' Declare new collection
        Dim myCollection = New Collection

        ' Create New Collection
        Set myCollection = New Collection

        ' Add items to collection
        myCollection.Add "John", "Name1"
        myCollection.Add "Maria", "Name2"
        myCollection.Add "Joseph", "Name3"

        ' Show the number of elements in collection
        MsgBox "Number of items in collection: & myCollection.Count

        ' Go through the elements of collection and display it into a
message box.
        Dim name As Variant
                For Each name In myCollection
                        MsgBox "Name": & name
                Next name

        ' Get an element of collection by key
        MsgBox "Name related with key 'Name2': " &
myCollection("Name2")

        ' Remove an element of collection by key
        Remove "Name1"

        ' Show the number of elements in collection after to remove an
element.
MsgBox " number of elements in collection after to remove an element.: &
myCollection.Count

End sub
```

28.80. Exercise number 80

Type: Concepts. The Nested With

Problem: Fill cells A1 through A500 with random values between 1 and 100. Then, apply a random background color and modify the text properties, such as font size, color, italics, bold, and underline. Use the 'with' method for nesting.

Solution: The 'with' method has been used on several occasions. This method allows for the reference to a single object without the need to repeat the object variable name multiple times. This approach avoids repetition and simplifies syntax.

Simple Solution:

The solution presented is the common and immediate one. The Font property is repeated seven times:

```
Option Explicit
_____

Sub withNoNested()

        With Range("A1:A500")

        .Interior.ColorIndex = WorksheetFunction.RandBetween (1, 50)
        .Value = WorksheetFunction.RandBetween (1, 100)
        .Font.Underline = True
        .Font. Bold = True
        .Font. Italic = True
        .Font. Color = RGB(0, 255, 10)
        .Font. Size = 15
        .Font.ThemeFont = xlThemeFontMajor

        End With
End Sub
```

The nested with code can simplify and enhance the above code's elegance.

With nested:

"With" statements can be nested or included inside each other. This approach offers the same result as with the non-nested "With," but with the advantages already discussed.

```vba
Option Explicit

Sub withNested()

        With Range("A1:A500")

        .Interior.ColorIndex = WorksheetFunction.RandBetween (1, 50)
        .Value = WorksheetFunction.RandBetween (1, 100)

                With .Font

                        'Properties of cells:
                        .Underline = True
                        .Bold = True
                        .Italic = True
                        .Color = RGB(0, 255, 10)
                        .Size = 15
                        .ThemeFont = xlThemeFontMajor

                End With
        End With
End Sub
```

28.81. Exercise number 81

Type: Concepts. Build policies

Problem: Perform a procedure that uses build constants. Using these constants, display the VBA version using a MsgBox.

Solution: Build constants in VBA are used to specify the version of the VBA language and other build options, such as the target platform. Predefined compiler constants in VBA include VBA6, VBA7, Win64, Win32, among others, and depend on the development platform, whether it is 16, 32, or 64-bit. These constants are used exclusively for #If...#Else instructions and are global in scope, meaning they apply to any location in a project.

```vba
Option Explicit


Sub constantsCompiler ( )

        #If VBA7 Then

        'This is Visual Basic 7
        MsgBox "Running in Visual Basic 7 or after"

                #Else
                        'specific code for production mode
                        MsgBox "Executing in bug mode"

        #End If

End Sub
```

28.82. Exercise number 82

Type: Concepts. Build policies

Problem: Use a constant of type #const to execute a specific piece of code depending on whether it is in debug mode or production mode.

Solution: Sometimes, it can be useful, particularly when delivering code to a client, to conduct a series of tests using real or simulated data to verify that the code is functioning correctly. These tests are typically performed in 'debug' mode.

In VBA, the #Const directive is different from other variables, which could change its value during code execution, constants have a fixed value that is determined at compile time and cannot be modified during program execution. The syntax of the #Const directive is as follows:

#Const ConstantName = Value

"*ConstantName*" is the name assigned to the constant and "*Value*" is the value that is also assigned to that constant. The value can be a text string, number, date, Boolean, or other.

#Const directives are used in conjunction with compilation directives #If...#Else...#End If, to conditionally compile specific parts of code based on the value of a compile-time constant. For instance, as previously mentioned, #Const can be employed to define a constant that determines the behavior of a particular piece of code depending on whether it is in debug mode or production mode.

```
Option Explicit
_____

'Assign one Boolean to variable
#Const bugMode = True

Sub myMacro ( )

        #If bugMode Then

        'specific code for bug mode
                MsgBox "Running in bug mode"

                    #Else
                            'specific code for production mode
                            MsgBox "Executing in bug mode"

        #End If

End Sub
```

28.83. Exercise number 83

Type: Concepts: GoSub

Problem: Perform a procedure that executes code, but at some point, it jumps to a later line of code executing new instructions and once finished, continues with what you were doing. Use the "GoSub" instruction and the use of tags.

Solution: The 'GoSub' instruction is used to jump to a different location in the code, specified by a label or line number within the current procedure, and then return to the previous position to continue with the execution of the code. If the 'GoSub' instruction were not known, there would be other similar solutions that could achieve the same result. However, it is useful to be aware of this possibility offered by VBA. This issue is resolved using 'GoSub'.:

```
Option Explicit


Public Sub OnGoSub ()

        MsgBox "I have come back!"

        GoSub Execute

        MsgBox "Hello World!"

        Exit Sub

Execute:

        MsgBox "I have executed"

        Return

End Sub
```

28.84. Exercise number 84

Type: Concepts: On... GoSub

Problem: Perform a procedure that executes code, but at specific points, it jumps to a later line of code executing new instructions and once finished, continues with what you were doing. Use the "On... GoSub" and using tags.

Solution: The On... GoSub statement is commonly utilized to jump to labels or line numbers based on the result of a numeric expression that evaluates a number between 0 and 255 (byte). Once the evaluation is complete, the code on this line or number is executed, and the statement can then return to the previous position using the 'Return' statement. The 'Select Case' statement is the most used form of branching.

```
Option Explicit


Public Sub OnGoSub ()

        Dim goTo As Byte
        goTo = 3

        On goTo GoSub step1, step2, step3
        MsgBox "I have come back"
        Exit Sub

        step1:
        MsgBox "Step1"
        Return

        Step2:
        MsgBox "Step2"
        Return

        Step3:
        MsgBox " Step3"
        Return

End Sub
```

I suggest that you modify the code by removing or commenting on the "return" of step2. You will notice that the code execution does not stop at that instruction, and goes to step3, ending there.

28.85. Exercise number 85

Type: Concepts: On... GoSub

Problem: Perform a procedure that executes code, but at specific points, it jumps to a later line of code executing new instructions and once finished, continues with what you were doing. To achieve this, use the 'On... GoSub' command and specify numerical values without labels.

Solution: The problem is like the previous one, but instead of using a tag, a number is used directly which could not correspond to the line of code.

```
Option Explicit


Public Sub OnGoSub ( )

            Dim goTo As Byte
            goTo = 3

            On goTo GoSub 55, 65, 75

            MsgBox "I have come back!"
            Exit Sub

55          MsgBox "Hello 55!"
            Return

65          MsgBox "Hello 65!"
            Return

75          MsgBox "Hello 75!"
            Return

End Sub
```

28.86. Exercise number 86

Type: Concepts: Wilds and the "like" operator

Problem: Determine if a text starts with the letter 'H', use a dialog box or MsgBox and use wildcards.

Solution: A wildcard (*) is a character used in text matching or search patterns to represent any other character or set of characters. The most used wildcard in VBA is the asterisk (*), which represents any number of characters (including zero characters) in a text string.

```
Option Explicit


Public Sub coincidence()
Dim text As String

text = "Hello Word"

            If text like "H*" then

                MsgBox "True"
                    Else
                        MsgBox "False"
                End if
End Sub
```

The code will return 'true' because 'Hello World' begins with 'H'. To check if it contains 'a', make the following modifications.

```vba
Option Explicit
```

```vba
Public Sub coincidence()
Dim text As String

text = "Hello Word"

        If text like "*a*" then

            MsgBox "True"
                Else
                    MsgBox "False"
            End if

End Sub
```

28.87. Exercise number 87

Type: Concepts: The Nothing

Problem: Declare an object variable named 'obj' without assigning any object to it. Then, use an 'if' statement to check whether it has been assigned to an object.

Solution: In VBA, the concept of 'Nothing' refers to a value that represents the absence of a valid object. It is helpful when assigning an object to a variable without referencing any object. 'Nothing' only works with objects.

```
Option Explicit


Sub exampleNothing()

        Dim obj As Object
        Dim value As Integer

        ' Declare obj as an object variable without assigning any object to
it
        ' This establishes it as Nothing

        If obj Is Nothing Then
                value = 0
                    Else
                        value = 1
        End If

        MsgBox " The value of the variable is: " & value

End Sub
```

28.88. Exercise number 88

Type: Concepts: The Nothing

Problem: In column A, create a list of fruits such as apples, bananas, oranges, pears, and others. Then, use a code to search for a specific fruit, such as 'orange', and determine if it exists or not.

	A
1	Pear
2	Banana
3	Apple
4	Orange
5	Kiwi
6	Pineapple

Solution: As previously mentioned, in VBA, the term 'Nothing' refers to a value that represents the absence of a valid object.

```
Option Explicit


Sub searchFruit( )

Dim ws Worksheet
Dim rngFruits Range
Dim fruitSearched As Range
Dim nameSearched As String

nameSearched = "Orange" 'Name of fruit searched

''Set worksheet and search range
Set ws = ThisWorkbook. Sheets ("Sheet1")
Set rngFruits = ws.Range("A:A") ' Range where you find the list of fruits

' Find the fruit in the range
Set fruitSearched = rngFruits.Find(nameSearched, LookIn:=xlValues,
LookAt:=xlWhole)

' Check if the fruit was found
If fruitSearched Is Nothing Then
```

```
        MsgBox " Fruit not found"  & nameSearched
              Else
                    MsgBox " Fruit found in the cell " & fruitSearched.Address

        End If

        ' Release memory occupied by objects
        Set ws = Nothing
        Set rngFruits = Nothing
        Set fruitSearched = Nothing

        End Sub
```

In this exercise, "Nothing" is used to initialize the fruitSearched variable before searching for the fruit's name in the range of cells in column A. If the "Orange" fruit is not found, the fruitSearched variable will remain as "Nothing", and can be checked with the If fruitSearched condition "Is Nothing" to display a message indicating that the fruit was not found.

Finally, to prevent memory leaks in your VBA code, it is important to free up the memory occupied by objects assigned to variables by using Set and setting them to Nothing when they are no longer needed.

28.89. Exercise number 89

Type: Concepts. Random

Problem: Generate a random number within a range of two values, one minimum and one maximum, by using the Randomize and Rnd functions. If, due to a user error, the minimum value is greater than the maximum, an error will be generated.

Solution: In VBA, the *Randomize* function initializes the random number generator with a "seed value". If no value is provided, the system clock is used to set this seed value by default. The Rnd function then generates random numbers based on the seed value set by *Randomize*.

However, while the *Rnd* function generates random numbers, the algorithm it uses is pseudorandom. This it means that the numbers it generates are determined by the seed value set by *Randomize*. If the same seed is set in different executions, the same sequence of random numbers will be generated.

Random number generation varies across operating systems and hardware. For example, Arduino which is a small computer, is known for its more reliable generation of random numbers compared to Excel's VBA.

The differences in random number generation between Arduino and Excel's VBA is due to the richer source of entropy used by Arduino. Unlike Excel's VBA, Arduino uses hardware inputs such as noise on analogical pins, fluctuations in temperature, magnetic fields, cosmic radiation, and other unpredictable events to generate a sequence of random numbers. These events are inherently unpredictable and constantly changing, resulting in a more random sequence of generated numbers.

On the other hand, Excel's VBA uses a pseudorandom algorithm for random number generation, which generates a sequence of random numbers based on an initial seed. Although these algorithms can produce sequences that appear random, the sequence is determined by the seed value and can be repeated if the same seed is used. Additionally, the quality of sequence randomness may depend on the specific algorithm used. Finally, you can use the following code:

```
Public Function createRandom(Minimum As Long, Maximum As Long) As
Long

' Check if the minimum value is greater than the maximum value
   If Minimum > Maximum Then
      Err.Raise  5 ' Raise an error if the minimum value is greater than the
maximum value
         Else
            Randomize  ' Initialize the random number generator
            'Calculate a random number within the specified range
            createRandom = Int((Maximum — Minimum + 1) * Rnd +
Minimum)
   End If

End Function
```

The code initially verifies that the first parameter is less than the second. It then calculates the length of the integer range between the minimum and maximum values, included. This length is multiplied by the result of the Rnd function, which generates a random number between 0 and 1. The outcome is added to the minimum value and truncated to an integer using the Int() function to obtain a random integer within the specified range.

28.90. Exercise number 90

Type: Concepts. Random

Problem: Perform a procedure that generates a sequence of random numbers using the "Rnd()" function and the "Randomize()" function, but they are always the same each time the procedure is executed.

Solution: The previous section discussed the seed value without using any arguments in either the 'Rnd' or the 'Randomize' functions.

The Rnd function generates a random number between 0 and 1 with a precision of 15 decimal digits. However, it may not generate enough random numbers on its own. To improve the results of Rnd, it is recommended to use the Randomize function before calling Rnd.

Rnd() argument:

- If the argument is negative, *Rnd* will return the same number each time the program runs.
- If the argument is zero, the Rnd function will return the last number generated by the Rnd function. If no number has been generated previously, the function will not return anything.
- If a positive argument is given or no argument is given at all, the function will return the next number in a sequence of pseudorandom numbers.

```
Debug.Print Rnd(-10) '0,3276443
Debug.Print Rnd(-1)  '0,224007
Debug.Print Rnd(0)   '0,224007
Debug.Print Rnd(1)   '3,584582E-02
Debug.Print Rnd(10)  '8,635235E-02
```

- *Randomize* does not return any values.
- If the 'randomize' function lacks arguments, it will use the current system time as a seed to initialize the random number generator.

- If a numeric argument is provided, it will always be used as the seed to initialize the random number generator.

After considering all the reasons, the solution to the problem is as follows: every time the code is executed, it will produce the same results.

```
Public Sub repeatResults()

        'With a negative argument we fix the results

        Debug.Print Rnd(-5) '0,8383257 print a fixed random number

        'With randomize we improve random results

        Debug.Print Rnd '0,9264714
        Debug.Print Rnd '0,3183454
        Debug.Print Rnd '0,319176

End Sub
```

28.91. Exercise number 91

Type: Concepts. Time and dates

Problem: Create a pop-up window that displays the current date and time.

Solution: To work with dates, there are three basic functions that is important to know. The first is the 'data' function, which returns the current date. The second is the 'Time' function, which returns the current time. Finally, the 'Now' function returns the current date and time at the same time.

```
Public Sub time_and_hour()

        MsgBox "Date is: " & Date & " and hour: " & Time
        MsgBox "But it is possible to get with: " & Now

End Sub
```

28.92. Exercise number 92

Type: Concepts. Time and dates

Problem: Convert a date in String format to date format.

Solution: In VBA, the "CDate" function can be used to convert a text string to a date. The syntax of the function is as follows: CDate(TextAsDate).

```
Sub transformToText ( )

        Dim dateText As String
        dateText = "30/04/2023"
        Range("A1").Value = CDate (dateText)

        If IsDate(dateText) Then

                MsgBox "It is a date"
                    Else
                            MsgBox "It is NOT a date"

        End if
End Sub
```

The 'TextDate' variable contains a text string representing a date in the day/month/year format. To convert this text string into an Excel date, the 'CDate' function is used, and the resulting date is displayed in cell A1. This step is crucial for performing date calculations, as the correct date format is required. Additionally, the 'isDate()' function is used to determine if the 'TextDate' is a date.

28.93. Exercise number 93

Type: Concepts. Time and dates

Problem: Use the previous example to display all dates formats in a range of cells.

Solution: To format the date 'datetext' in all Excel VBA formats, use the 'Format' function. This feature enables you to format a date based on the specified format string.

```
Sub transformToText ()

Dim dateText As String
dateText = "30/04/2023"
Range ("A1").Value = CDate (dateText)

If IsDate(dateText) Then

        MsgBox "It is a date"
            Else
                MsgBox "It is not a date"
End If

        Range("A2").Value = Format (dateText, "dd/mm/yyyy")
        Range("A3").Value = Format (dateText , "dd-mm-yyyy")
        Range("A4").Value = Format (dateText, "dd.mm.yyyy")
        Range("A5").Value = Format (dateText, "dd/mm/yy")
        Range("A6").Value = Format (dateText, "dd-mm-yy")
        Range("A7").Value = Format (dateText, "dd.mm.yy")
        Range("A8").Value = Format (dateText, "mmm dd, yyyy")
        Range("A9").Value = Format (dateText, "mmmm dd, yyyy")
        Range("A10").Value = Format (dateText, "dddd, mmmm dd, yyyy")
        Range("A11").Value = Format (dateText, "dd/mm/yyyy
hh:mm:ss")

End Sub
```

28.94. Exercise number 94

Type: Concepts. Time and dates

Problem: Create a program in Excel VBA that allows for a brief pause. Use the 'Timer' function.

Solution: The 'Timer' function retrieves the current time in seconds. A 'Do While' loop is then implemented to pause the program until the current time is X seconds greater than the initial time.

```vba
Option Explicit


Public Sub timeSleepProcedure ()
        MsgBox "I Sleep: " & sleep(4) & " seconds."
End Sub


Function sleep (seconds As Long) As Long

        Dim startTime As Single
        startTime = Timer

        Do While (Timer – startTime) < seconds
        'Waiting
        Loop

sleep = seconds

End Function
```

The Application.Wait statement (Now + TimeValue("0:00:04")) can also be used to pause the execution of the code for four seconds.

```vba
Sub sleepFewSeconds()

        Application.Wait (Now + TimeValue ("0:00:04"))

End Sub
```

28.95. Exercise number 95

Type: Concepts. Time and dates

Problem: Run a procedure periodically using the *"Application.OnTime"* method.

Solution: To execute a procedure after a specific time interval, the 'Application.OnTime' method can be used. Although alternative methods exist, VBA provides a straightforward solution.

```vba
Option Explicit


Public Sub runJobs()

        Application.OnTime Now + TimeValue ("00:00:04"),
"runProcedure"

End Sub


Public Sub runProcedure()

        MsgBox "Good Morning!"

End Sub
```

28.96. Exercise number 96

Type: Concepts. The Assert

Problem: Use the "*debug*" object and the *"Assert"* method, to determine if the following statements are true: five is greater than four and ten is less than five. If the expression is true, proceed with running the code. Otherwise, interrupt the execution. Additionally, interrupt the execution with a zero and null.

Solution: The *"Debug.Assert"* is used to verify that a specific expression or condition is true during program execution. If the expression is false or null, the program will halt, and an error message will be displayed to assist in debugging.

```
Public Sub debugAssert()

        Debug.Assert 5 > 4
        Debug.Assert 10 < 5
        Debug.Assert 0
        Debug.Assert Null

End Sub
```

The *Debug.Assert* statement is a valuable debugging tool used to identify errors in your code and ensure that specific conditions are met during program execution. *Debug.Assert* requires an expression that should be true, and if it is false, null, or zero, the program will halt and display an error message to aid in debugging.

28.97. Exercise number 97

Type: Concepts. The Stop

Problem: Write a program that sums the values of the selected cells into a range. But if one of the cells contains "Stop" text, the code execution stops.

Solution: To stop the execution of a program in Excel VBA, the 'Stop' statement can be used. This statement can be inserted at any point into the code when the program needs to be stopped.

The following code iterates through all cells of range in the active sheet and halt the program execution if the keyword 'stop' is encountered.

```
Sub stop_program ( )

Dim myCell As Range
Dim sum As Double

For Each myCell In ActiveSheet.UsedRange

        If myCell.Value = "stop" Then
           Stop  'Program halted due to "stop" keyword
              Else
                  Sum = sum + myCell.Value
        End if

Next myCell
MsgBox sum

End Sub
```

28.98. Exercise number 98

Type: Concepts. Name shading

Problem: Generate a "Name Shadowing" case by creating a procedure in a module and defining a local and global variable named "myVariable".

Solution: *"Name shadowing"* in VBA is the act of defining both a local and global variable, or an object in the Excel object library with the same name.

```vba
Public myVariable as Integer

Sub myShadow()

    Dim myVariable As String
    myVariable = "this is String"

End Sub
```

In this case, the local variable "myVariable" shades the global variable of the same name. When "myVariable" is referenced within the "myShadow" procedure, the local variable is being referenced instead of the global variable. Therefore, any operation performed on "myVariable" within "myShadow" will only affect the local variable and not the global variable.

To avoid name shading issues, it is good practice to use unique and descriptive variable names throughout your VBA project. Another solution is to fully qualify the variable name. To do this, include the name of the module in which the variable is declared, followed by the dot operator ("."), followed by the name of the variable.

For example: *module1.variablePublic*

28.99. Exercise number 99

Type: Concepts. Parameterized Procedures

Problem: Perform a procedure that receives two integer values as an argument, sums them, and displays them on the screen.

Solution: The task is to program a procedure that takes two integer arguments, such as *num1* and *num2*, and displays the result. To accomplish this, a 'Main' procedure can be written to call the *'sum'* procedure with values obtained from the user using the 'InputBox' function. The user's input values are then passed as arguments to the 'Add' procedure by calling it with add *num1* and *num2*.

```
Option Explicit


Sub sum(ByVal num1 As Integer, ByVal num2 As Integer)

        Dim result As Integer
        result = num1 + num2
        MsgBox "The result is: " & result

End Sub


Sub main ()

        Dim value1 As Integer
        Dim value2 As Integer

        value1 = InputBox ("First value:")
        value2 = InputBox ("Second value:")

        value1 = Int(value1)
        value2 = Int(value2)

        sum value1, value2

End Sub
```

Up to this exercise, the procedures we have studied have not yet incorporated arguments. However, as demonstrated in this exercise, by defining a procedure as either a 'Sub' or a 'Function', you can provide arguments in the order specified in the procedure definition or, alternatively, using named arguments.

28.100. Exercise number 100

Type: Concepts. Parameterized Procedures

Problem: Repeat the previous problem, but now using named arguments.

Solution: Named arguments can be useful when dealing with a vast number of parameters, particularly when calling procedures with optional parameters. Additionally, it enhances the traceability of past and omitted arguments.

```
Option Explicit

Sub sum(ByVal num1 As Integer, ByVal num2 As Integer, ByVal num3 As
Integer, ByVal num4 As Integer)

        Dim result As Integer
        result = num1 + num2 + num3 + num4
        MsgBox "The result of addition is: " &result

End Sub

Sub main()

        Dim value1 As Integer
        Dim value2 As Integer
        Dim value3 As Integer
        Dim value4 As Integer

        value1 = InputBox("Insert first value: ")
        value2 = InputBox("Insert second value: ")
        value3 = InputBox("Insert third value: ")
        value4 = InputBox("Insert fourth value: ")

        value1 = Int(value1)
        value2 = Int(value2)
        value3 = Int(value3)
        value4 = Int(value4)

        sum num1:=value1, num2:=value2, num3:=value3, num4:=value4
```

End Sub

In the example provided, four arguments are used to demonstrate that the order of the arguments does not affect the result or cause errors if the parameter is named correctly and followed by a colon with an equal sign (:=).

29.REFERENCES

[1]. Develop solutions and customize Excel: https://learn.microsoft.com/es-es/office/client-developer/excel/excel- home?redirectedfrom=MSDN

[2]. Personal notes and notes

[3]. MS Excel. VBA Reference for Excel: https://learn.microsoft.com/es-es/office/vba/api/overview/excel

[4]. Technology, programming, and computer web. Specialists in mobile application development, solutions for microcontrollers and automations:
https://www.joober.eu

30.KEYWORDS

VBA, Visual, Basic, Applications, Excel, developer, computer, computer, algorithm, programming, classes, objects, macro, properties, methods, record, cell, functions, lookup, activecell, offset, filter, for, next, OnKey, set, each, While, Loop, Do, members, UserForm, label, ComboBox, RefEdit, ThisWorkbook, ActiveX, arguments, parameters, ByVal, bit, byte, octet, hexadecimal, binary, languages, code, ASCII, form, String, procedures, module, RefEditCtrl, sub, ByRef, intersect, Colouring, variable, Ubound, games, pong, telepong, API

31. VBA EXCEL PROGRAMMING

This practical book is recommended for developers and Excel users who want to learn how to work with VBA effectively and enjoyably. It covers basic programming concepts as well as advanced techniques.

Visual Basic for Excel is a powerful tool that enables you to automate tasks, create custom macros, and enhance spreadsheet capabilities.

This book teaches you how to write clear, concise, and readable code to simplify tasks and create efficient spreadsheets.

Through practical examples, games, and detailed explanations, this book will guide you through the main concepts of VBA for Excel, including:

- The fundamentals of VBA programming.
- How to use the Visual Basic editor to create and modify macros.
- How to work with conditional variables and loops to control the flow of code.
- How to use functions and subroutines to create custom macros.
- How to work with Excel objects to interact with spreadsheets and other items.
- How to design forms and pop-ups.
- How to use APIs.
- Games and much more!

32. THE AUTHOR

Josep R. Vidal Bosch was born in Barcelona, Europe in 1984. He graduated from the Universitat Politècnica de Catalunya and Universidad Politècnica de Cartagena in Naval Architecture & Marine Engineering. He has developed his professional activity in one of the most significant docks in Southern Europe and has participated in various underwater naval construction projects, electronic engineering projects related to microcontrollers (Arduino, Raspberry Pi, Beaglebone Black), robotics, mobile apps, and website development.

33. COMMENTS & REVIEWS

Finally, whether you loved this book or had mixed feelings about it, I would appreciate your **honest review**. Your feedback helps me, to improve and assists other readers in making informed decisions. Thank you for taking your time to share your thoughts.

www.ingramcontent.com/pod-product-compliance
Lightning Source LLC
LaVergne TN
LVHW051426050326
832903LV00030BD/2942